Tools for the
Recovery of Body, Mind,
Heart & Soul

The Healing Runes

Commentary by

Ralph H. Blum
and
Susan Loughan

St. Martin's Press ✶ *New York*

Also by Ralph H. Blum

The Book of Runes
The Book of Runes Tenth Anniversary Edition
The Book of RuneCards
Rune Play

Edited by Bill Mason
Design by Jaye Zimet

Library of Congress Cataloging-in-Publication Data
Blum, Ralph.
    The healing runes   :   tools for the recovery of body, mind, heart &
  soul   /   Ralph H. Blum & Susan Loughan : preface by Thomas Moore.
      p.   cm.
    "A Thomas Dunne book."
    ISBN 0-312-13507-6
    1. Runes—Miscellanea.   2. Mental healing.   I. Loughan, Susan.
  II. Title.
  BF575L3B57   1995
  133.3'3—dc20   95-24221
                                                      CIP

10 9 8 7 6 5 4 3 2

For Jeanne Elizabeth Blum. Your courage, grace and wisdom are heaven's blessing on my life.

For Alan B. Slifka, Founder of the Abraham Fund, whose insightful generosity has modeled, in the world, pathways for healing the world.

For Martin and Penny Rayner, who taught me to feel the water and watch the wind.

And for all of us whose personal human programs are infected by a virus that makes us believe we are less than we are. This book is dedicated to the elimination of that virus.

—RHB

This book is dedicated to God and to the great teachers of my life.

To my mother, Ruth Torbett Loughan, for teaching me the passion of faith.

To my daughter, Wende Williams, for teaching me how to love.

To Erica Knowles, one of the wisest of my teachers.

To Brad Davis and Joseph Runningfox, for teaching me how to fly.

—SL

Contents

Invocation   *vi*
Preface by Thomas Moore   *vii*
Introductions   *xiii*

1—A Legacy of Healing from the Ancient World   3
2—A Brief History of the Runes   9
3—In Praise of the Oracular   17
4—Using the Healing Runes   23
5—Healing Rune Spreads   39
6—A Circle of Healing Runes   55
7—Rune Interpretations   71
8—Pastoral Authority   125
9—New Runes for Old Friends   129

Envoi: Thoughts for the Soul   133
Acknowledgments   137
Selected Bibliography   145
About the Authors   153
The RuneWorks   155

Invocation

I beseech Thee to grant me the grace
to continue in Thy presence.

—Brother Lawrence

Practice the Presence of God in all ways,
Both in your coming in and your going out.
In your prayers, invoke God's Presence.
In your aspirations, stay mindful of the Presence.
In your meditations, breathe in the Presence.
Above all, let the Presence be reflected in your
  attitude,
For surely then God will sing in your thoughts,
Speak in your voice and shine through your acts.
Let the Presence of God be the medicine
To heal your life, lift your heart and renew your
  spirit.

Practice the Presence of God in all ways,
Both in your coming in and your going out.

—RHB

Preface
by Thomas Moore

It is the human condition to be in need of healing, for we are not, not any of us, fully sound, fit and hale in body and soul. So, an essential part of our lives must be dedicated to some kind of "medicine," in the best sense of the word. The trouble in modern times is that we pursue healing piecemeal and incompletely. We separate, each from the other, the sicknesses of body, emotion, meaning and connectedness. We have a tendency to trust both the mind and machinery too much, thinking that if we could only understand the basis of our distress, we might make it right, or if we could find the best expert having the newest technologies, then we might possess the elusive elixir of physical and emotional health.

People who live or have lived outside the bubble of modern sensibilities look upon illness and healing differently. The ancient Greeks would make a sacrifice at the temple of the healing god Aesculapius and spend the night in hope of a cure. Some communities today consult a diviner or a shamanic medicine person who knows herbs and dreams. Modern people sometimes try to borrow folk techniques and medicines, but we know that we can't just suddenly go primitive and pretend that modern medicine and therapy never happened. Our challenge is to become aware of serious holes in our approach to healing ourselves, learn from as many sources as possible how we might re-vision our methods and attitudes, and then develop newly animated ways of healing.

We realize that we need insight, especially in disturbances of the soul—addictions, depressions, emotional upheaval, relationship breakdowns, all kinds of acting out—and so we flock to therapists and buy books that tell us what we're doing wrong and how to get back on track. But I suspect that our quest for insight doesn't go nearly deep enough. It isn't sufficient to cling to a new theory or therapy that promises salvation from soul distress. We have to live daily from a deeper place, thereby healing many of the divisions in vision and philosophy that lie at the heart of our wounds. It is in this search for deeper insight that *The Healing Runes* of Ralph Blum and Susan Loughan can guide us.

We need nothing less than a revolution in our ways of knowing and understanding. In modern life we tend to turn everything into a mental issue. In sports we like to discuss statistics, instead of enjoying athletics. In education we stuff the brain with facts, instead of addressing ways of understanding things we cannot quantify. In psychotherapy we look for causes and explanations, instead of seeking ways to heal the individual soul. To ease the anxiety and distress of modern times we need to deepen our knowledge to a point beyond mere explanation, to a place where the soul is moved and therefore touched and healed.

I used to think that intuition was the answer, and that we could somehow squeeze brilliant ideas from this neglected organ of the mind. Now, I've learned that intuition is not a mental activity at root but a posture in the world and a method of knowing that offers guidance to the soul, even as it fails to satisfy the mind's longing for clear and unambiguous explanations.

I've learned that real intuition requires skills and attitudes that are more demanding than those of the mind; it demands some concrete object, image or ritual procedure, and it doesn't act in a vacuum. It presents no sure knowledge, but rather offers information that is poetic in nature, and often ambiguous, ambivalent, paradoxical, and elusive. Its answers to our problems are neither immediate nor fully conclusive, but rather take time to unfold and may never stand fully revealed.

Because the knowledge that rises out of the intuition—and out of the oracular—is so deep-seated, it appears to belong more in the realm of religion than psychology, and so some people are hesitant to approach it lest they transgress their beliefs and theological convictions. We are all influenced, too, by Western religion's long suspicions about paganism, superstition and magical practices. Study after study has shown that the churches make careful distinctions about oracles. They seem to be most interested in protecting the notion of free will for humans, and divine freedom as well. They resist a kind of magical universe in which certain actions automatically and necessarily produce effects, and they warn against any individual's taking personal advantage of that magic.

Yet, the oracular is an integral part of all religions, from the Greeks consulting the oracle at Delphi, to the Priests of the Old Testament dedicated to reading the signs of nature, to St. Augustine. In his *Confessions*, Augustine asserts his love of the oracular and tells the moving story of how, in the midst of his agony over the disastrous way his life had gone, he heard a child's voice telling him to read. So he picked up a Bible and read the first words that presented themselves to him. He describes this as a technique—divining the passage that will set a meaningful life course. The words he read advised him against a wasted life, and taking them to heart, he embraced an altogether new direction, becoming a bishop, theologian and saint.

As oracular tools, the Runes provide a way of deepening reflection and stirring the soul where it counts, where meaning coalesces and emotions find their place. This is indeed the edge of religion, but think of what the Runes do in the medieval view of philosophy, as servants to theology. There need be no conflict, but rather, the one can ground the other.

Ralph Blum does us the great service of offering this new set of Interpretations for the Runes. He and Susan Loughan do so in graceful and appropriate language. Their words could set in motion our own individual reflections and reverie, leading to a kind of knowledge that is solid, like the stone the alchemists sought, and poetic, like the colorful peacock's tail they saw as an emblem for the multifaceted soul.

I am convinced that all healing ultimately comes from a shift in deep imagination, and this is what the Runes do when read sensitively, as in this edition: They ground the interpretations of our own lives and anchor our decisions in the very quick of the heart.

If we suffer from any universal disease, it is shallowness of imagination. *The Healing Runes* offers a remedy for that malady. In so doing, it promises not just relief from anxiety, but profound gifts that signal the presence of soul—intimacy, pleasure, beauty, love and piety.

Evoking the Soul

Until one is committed, there is hesitancy, the chance to draw back, always ineffectiveness. Concerning all acts of initiative there is one elementary truth, the ignorance of which kills countless ideas and splendid plans: that the moment one definitely commits oneself, then Providence moves too.

All sorts of things occur to help one that would otherwise never have occurred. A whole stream of events issues from the decision, raising in one's favor all manner of incidents and meetings and material assistance which no person would have believed would have come their way. Whatever you think you can do or believe you can do, begin it. Action has magic, grace and power in it.

—Goethe

Introduction
—Ralph H. Blum

Although I did not realize it when I wrote the Commentary for *The Book of Runes*,* I was creating my own personal guidebook. A guidebook to becoming a more conscious human being and taking greater responsibility for my life.

The letters I have received over the years, from people who use the Runes as a self-counseling tool, have taught me a powerful lesson: Something so personal to me could be usefully applied to the lives of people around the world. And when one person's words resonate in the hearts of so many, it demonstrates how deeply connected we are to each other. We all share the same goals. We make up one community, one fellowship.

The Book of Runes was a gift to myself to facilitate my own spiritual healing. Now I am in the process of emotional healing. This new work is for all of you who have chosen to travel the same road.

---

*The Book of Runes, published in 1982 by St. Martin's Press, was intended to serve as "an instrument for learning the will of God in our lives."

The Runes themselves are of Germanic and Norse origin, an ancient alphabetic script, each of whose letters possessed a meaningful name as well as a signifying sound. In their time Runes were employed for legal documents, for writing poetry, for inscriptions and as an Oracle for communicating with the Divine. The Runes were in general use until the end of the twelfth century. (See Chapter 2: "A Brief History of the Runes.")

Recently, I found myself at a place in my life where I had no choice but to become honest with myself and with others. Through the years, it became obvious to me that many of the people who attended my lectures and seminars were considerably further along than I was in the process of self-understanding and healing. In the past, I might have felt threatened by that recognition. Yet it was when I came to see these people as a source of inspiration that I realized I was truly ready to change.

I spent many years trying to heal by developing my spiritual understanding before I came to recognize the importance of facing the emotional and psychological problems rooted in my childhood. Like so many people in the seventies and early eighties, I chose to see and manage my issues through spiritual eyes—to rise above and transcend them. It didn't quite work. Coming out of denial was one of the most difficult things I've ever had to do. In the early 1990s, I was working very hard at bottoming out.

Then I attended my first Twelve Step meeting. As time went on, I was drawn to a variety of Twelve Step programs that were all disturbingly relevant to my life. I discovered in the early weeks I spent attending meetings that, even by the most rigorous of criteria, I qualified in at least *five* major addictive diseases.

So I kept coming back. It was in those meetings that I found people who talked me through the night and nourished me and listened.

Through working the Program, and through the caring support of friends and the abiding love of my wife, Jeanne, I came to recognize in myself a fierce hunger to reconnect with the depth and complexity of my feelings.

After forty years of studying the world's oracular systems,

I am convinced that we all share a profound need to look deeply into ourselves; to go beyond the stories we tell about why we are the way we are; to find our own truth and, acting upon that truth, take on the divinely appointed tasks we are here to perform.

In 1992, when I was working on the Tenth Anniversary Edition of *The Book of Runes*, Susan Loughan came to me and suggested a new project. Because of her years of experience in a variety of Twelve Step programs, Susan wanted to provide a healing tool based on the Runes—a reinterpretation to supplement Recovery programs and other forms of traditional therapy.

And yet I was troubled. Although I recognized the value of her idea immediately, I was uncertain whether or not to go ahead. I had already taken a 2,000-year-old alphabet, changed the order of its letters and adapted its ancient oracular meanings for the modern world. By then, a great many people had already consulted *The Book of Runes*, using the Interpretations to support their choices and track their actions. Did I, I asked myself, have the right to undertake *another* adaptation of the original Runes?

My friend Thorsten Orlikowsky, M.D., an immunologist from the German University of Tübingen and a preeminent runic scholar, encouraged me. He said: "As we know, life presents itself simultaneously on three levels—the spiritual, the emotional and the physical. With *The Book of Runes*, you addressed the spiritual level. This is an opportunity to *progress* the meanings of the Runes to support people in their emotional and physical healing. It is the natural next step for your work."

After talking with Thorsten, I realized I could go forward with this book without compromising the integrity of the ancient Oracle.

I now firmly believe it was God's will that I undertake this project. We are a world in crisis, a world filled with pain and suffering. The major issue of our time is the healing of our planet and all its people. To that end, *The Healing Runes* is dedicated.

During the writing of *The Healing Runes,* two issues have come up again and again for me: my relationship to God, and the expression of my feelings about that relationship as they appear in these pages. This book is as much about healing our connection with the Divine as it is about other kinds of healing. Working a Twelve Step Program and collaborating with Susan have renewed my sensitivity to the healing power of faith.

Nevertheless, in reading through the completed Interpretations for *The Healing Runes,* I became concerned over how often we had mentioned the Divine. I had to ask myself: Are these pages too saturated with God? Is it a burden upon those who recognize a Higher Power, yet flinch and recoil from any attempt to "name the unnamable"?

So, in answer to the latter question, I am heartened and encouraged by the approach taken by Larry Dossey, M.D., in his outstanding book, *Healing Words: The Power of Prayer and the Practice of Medicine,* where he speaks of the Divine as "the Absolute." In addressing the issue of the feminine face of the Divine, he clears away more of the underbrush:

> At this moment in history, in which we're experiencing a much-needed awakening of feminine values, perhaps it is important to point out that the problem of naming the Absolute is not resolved merely by replacing all the masculine names and pronouns with feminine ones. The Absolute is radically beyond any description

whatsoever, including gender. With these limitations in mind, the reader may insert, in every instance that follows, his or her preferred name for the Absolute—whether the Great Spirit, Goddess, God, Allah, Krishna, Brahman, the Tao, the Universal Mind, the Almighty, Alpha and Omega, the One.*

I submit that we all owe much to Dr. Dossey for his clarification. With him, I welcome all names for the Divine.

And besides, can there be "too much" God? What else is there but God? To have God as we understand God, in all our daily thoughts and acts and words, is to recognize the truth about our nature.

The oracular is but one sacred means, among so many others, for God to speak to us. In 1988, I wrote: "People all over this country, from all walks of life, are experiencing an intense desire to be filled by Spirit. We are being moved to become, in our own right, oracular voices for a Power greater than ourselves." It is Susan's and my hope that *The Healing Runes* will play its part in celebrating the Voice of the Divine in our daily lives.

---

*Larry Dossey, M.D., *Healing Words: The Power of Prayer and the Practice of Medicine* (San Francisco: Harper SanFrancisco, 1993).

Introduction
—Susan Loughan

I'm finally at a place in my life where it's time to look back. Ever since my dear friend Julia Adams introduced me to them long ago, the Runes have been my good friends. Now, they have become one of the final pieces I needed to complete my healing journey—the stimulus for collaborating on this book.

Writing this book with Ralph has been a powerful, sometimes difficult, always stimulating experience. *The Healing Runes* is an attempt to strike a balance: to draw upon the gifts I have received during my thirty years as a healer and give something back.

Sometimes we lose our way before we find ourselves. *The Healing Runes* is a compass to guide us on our return to wholeness. One thing is certain: That journey is different for each of us. For some, it is a chosen path; for others, it is part of a struggle to stay alive.

It is through hard work and faith, and a need to strengthen our spirits, that we take our healing and our recovery out into the world to serve and inspire others. In the past, each time I felt I just couldn't go on, I would think of what my clients have been through, survived and overcome. As a healer, so many times I've heard myself saying: "Don't give up. Don't *ever* give up." Again and again, life has taught me that adversity can be as healing as joy and happiness.

Robin Norwood's work is a wonderful example of the inspiration to never give up. In her book *Why Me, Why This,*

Why Now, she talks about the power of adversity, and how people are so often afraid of the very things that can heal them. Norwood writes: "We can trust not only that the pain will pass, but that our suffering has meaning and purpose and dignity."*

It is my hope that the Healing Runes will serve us all in getting back to basics. Forgiveness is a basic. Courage and Gratitude and Compassion and Humor are basics. If we are to heal, we need to restore what is basic to our nature and thus to our lives.

In thinking about the lives of those who have come to me seeking counsel, two stories come to mind. I remember a powerful woman named Beatrice, an athlete dying of AIDS. She hoped I might help her recover a lost part of herself, a part that would allow the inner peace she sought in the face of death. One day, she asked me how I had survived the sorrows of my own life. For some reason, I broke into uncontrollable laughter. Before I could stop, we were both laughing. Then we both began to cry, and in that moment, through the tears, I blurted out: "Compassion! That's the piece you're looking for! When you are able to give it to yourself, you will see the world through loving eyes." A few weeks later, at peace with her life, Beatrice died.

Compassion is the twenty-fourth Healing Rune. Serenity, Faith, Fear, Surrender, Trust—let each one of the twenty-five Runes accompany you on your healing journey.

In conclusion, let me tell you a story that still touches my

---

*Robin Norwood, *Why Me, Why This, Why Now: A Guide to Answering Life's Toughest Questions* (New York: Carol Southern Books, 1994).

life profoundly. Many years ago, a woman named Dara came to me seeking insight on her most extraordinary life. Fifteen years before, she had been in a near-fatal car accident and burned over 75 percent of her body. At our first meeting, I was struck by the power of her presence, her acceptance of what had happened and the magnitude of her physical beauty. Somehow, at a very young age, she possessed the knowledge that her accident was, indeed, part of a larger plan. It was this knowledge that forever aligned me to the power and strength of the human spirit. Dara's life is proof of the healing power of God's love in all of our lives.

Beatrice, Dara and all my clients over the years planted in me seeds that would one day flower in these pages.

Prayer

Holy Spirit,
Giving life to all life,
Moving all creatures,
Root of all things,
Washing them clean,
Wiping out their mistakes,
Healing their wounds,
You are our true life,
Luminous, wonderful,
Awakening the heart
From its ancient sleep.

—Hildegard of Bingen
(A.D. 1098–1179)

A Legacy of Healing from the Ancient World

Health is a state of complete physical, mental and social well-being, and not merely the absence of disease and infirmity.

—The World Health Organization

The body cannot be cured without regard for the soul.

—Socrates (c. 470–399 B.C.)

It is true that many cultures around the globe have contributed to our healing legacy, but cataloguing their contributions is not the purpose of this work. We are concerned here with the way the healing journey leads to the oracular, and hence to the Runes.

For many thousands of years, possibly back to the beginning of recorded time, humanity has welcomed all forms of healing. The philosophy has always been: *If it helps, heals, cures or reduces pain, use it.* Now, Western medicine has begun to explore the wisdom and knowledge of the shamans of the rain forests, the Siberian taiga, the Native American medicine people. Medical practitioners, specialists and ordinary people from every culture in the world—including, it is estimated, *one-third of all Americans*—now accept and practice some form of alternative medicine.

More and more, the Western medical establishment is coming to understand that the way we live our lives, and the quality of our thoughts and emotions, affects our spiritual, emotional, mental and physical disposition toward illness or toward health. From the Tao, as from the Greek oracle at Delphi, we hear the teaching: "Know thyself." The power of those two words has no equal.

Chi

Nowadays, we hear considerable talk about energy and energy medicine, and about a mysterious force known as *chi*. None of this, journalist Bill Moyers reminds us in his groundbreaking book *Healing and the Mind*, is new. To the Chinese, as well as to their physicians,

> the body is a series of energy conduits. *Chi*, the Chinese name for this energy, flows along systematic [lines or] meridians, which do not coincide with any known physiological structures. When a patient is ill, our Western doctors look for physical or chemical abnormalities. Chinese doctors search for hidden forces that are out of balance. Their task, as they describe it, is to restore unseen harmonies. Sticking needles into the body is obviously a physical intervention to Westerners, but not to the Chinese. They see it as intervening in an energy system. Through pressing needles

into specific points in the body . . . and massaging pressure points, Chinese doctors, it is said, control the flow of *chi*.*

With the growing acceptance of acupuncture and acupressure among Western medical practitioners, such terms as *"chi,"* "pressure points" and "meridians" are now moving from alternative to mainstream status.

Incubation

In ancient Egypt, people traditionally slept within temple precincts hoping for a therapeutic dream through which to be healed from an illness.

To seek healing through this process was later made known throughout Western Europe by the Greeks and Romans who called it "incubation." The sick, or those who sought spiritual advice, gathered in the temples for the priests to diagnose or counsel them. People coming to experience incubation or "temple sleep" were visited by priests who gave advice, often through the interpretation of their dreams, for such dreams were regarded as oracular pronouncements, word from the gods. It can be fairly said that, in temple sleep, the patient is the Oracle.

---

*Bill Moyers, *Healing and the Mind* (New York: Doubleday, 1993).

Miracles

"In your consideration of alternative healing, don't neglect Scripture," said my friend, the Reverend Wallace K. Reid, a retired Baptist minister. "For my money, there is no higher form of alternative healing than a miracle." Consider Elijah bringing a dead boy back to life in I Kings 17:17–24, or the sight of Jesus healing a leper in Matthew 8:2–4. Jesus' compassion for humanity is expressed in John 14:12, in a promise made not only to the disciples but also to the following generations of believers, the promise that "They that believe in me, the works that I do they shall do also; and greater works than these shall they do."

When a terminal illness, like cancer, spontaneously disappears, there is no explanation, and we tend to speak of a "miraculous cure." It is against this background of ancient healing traditions that we can best appreciate the healing side of the oracular.

Welsh Rune

In this fateful hour,
I call upon all Heaven with its power
And the sun with its brightness
And the snow with its whiteness
And the fire with all the strength it hath
And the lightning with its rapid wrath
And the winds with their swiftness along the path
And the sea with its deepness
And the rocks with their steepness
And the earth with its starkness.
All these I place,
By Heaven's almighty help and grace,
Between myself and the powers of darkness.

—Traditional

A Brief History
of the Runes

2

The word "rune" suggests not merely a form of writing, the angular characters of the old Germanic script long since discarded, but a whole world of mystery. . . . When Bishop Wulfila translated the Bible into fourth-century Gothic, he rendered St. Mark's "the mystery of the kingdom of God" (using runa *for mystery). When the chieftains and wise counselors of Anglo-Saxon England gathered in conclave, men called their secret deliberations "runes."*

—Ralph W. V. Elliott
RUNES: AN INTRODUCTION

Whenever you can, let people know what tradition you are working with. And if they are part of it, show that to them. After all, it makes sense to be interested in and feel respect for what is part of your inheritance.

—Margaret Mead

An aura of mystery will always surround the origins and sacred use of the Runes, an alphabetic script used by the ancient Germanic and Norse peoples. According to tradition, the Runes were Odin's gift to humanity. Odin was the principal deity in the pantheon of the Norse gods. His name derives from the Old Norse for "wind" and "spirit." In the legend,

9

Odin hung for nine nights and days on *Yggdrasil*, the Tree of the World, wounded by his own blade, tormented by hunger, thirst and pain, unaided and alone until he spied the Runes, and with a tremendous effort seized them up.

The Origins of the Runes

There is no firm agreement among scholars as to when and where runic writing first made its appearance in Western Europe. During the centuries—millennia perhaps—before the Germanic tribal peoples possessed any form of alphabet or alphabetic script, they made ceremonial and propitiatory use of pictorial glyphs or symbols that they scratched or carved onto rocks. Dating from the second Bronze Age (circa 1300 to 1200 B.C.) and from the period of transition to the Iron Age (circa 800 to 600 B.C.), the majority of these prehistoric rock carvings or *hällristningar*, is thought to be linked to groups of Indo-European fertility and sun worshippers. The most common symbols found in the rock carvings include representations of human and animal forms, parts of the human body, weapon motifs, swastikas, sun symbols, swirls, wheels and other variations on square and circular forms.

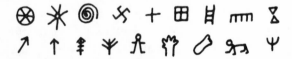

The creation of the runic script began when these pre-runic pictorial symbols melded with elements of the already existing Latin, Greek, Etruscan and Northern Italic alphabets. Evidence to support the timing of this fusion comes from several related alphabets used in inscriptions found in the Alps and dating from the fourth to the first century B.C.

In his fine book, *Runes: An Introduction*, Ralph W. V. Elliott comments on the amalgamation of these two separate traditions, "the alphabetic script on the one hand, the symbolic content on the other," indicating that whoever invented the runic alphabet had to be familiar with the pre-runic symbols. Elliott writes: "All we know is that in some Germanic tribe some man had both the leisure (a factor often forgotten) and the remarkable phonetic sense to create the [runic alphabet] from a North Italic model known to him somewhere in the alpine regions in the period circa 250 to 150 B.C."*

Another runic scholar, an English friend of mine, puts it somewhat cynically: "It's really quite simple. At that time, those German tribal chaps were running around naked, painting themselves blue and driving the Romans batty. So someone came up with the clever idea of giving them an alphabet to keep them out of mischief."

There is considerable agreement among runic scholars that, from its very inception, runic writing was not primarily utilitarian, and that the evidence of its sacred function is found first in the bonding of secular letters with the pre-runic symbols employed in pagan Germanic rites and religious practices and, even more dramatically, in their association

---

*Ralph W. V. Elliott, *Runes: An Introduction* (Manchester: Manchester University Press, 1959). There are a number of useful books on the Runes, but I recommend this one in particular: If your appetite for runology is whetted, see Elliott's Selected Bibliography, or the Selected Bibliography in *The Book of Runes*.

with the Germanic gods, thereby situating the runic alphabet at the very heart of the old Germanic religion.

To the pagan mind, the earth and all created things were alive. Twigs and stones served for Rune casting since, as natural objects, they were believed to embody the sacred. Over the centuries, Runes have been carved into pieces of hardwood, incised on metal or cut into leather. The most common Runes would have been short sticks or smooth, flat pebbles with the symbols marked on one side.

We have scant information as to who cut the Runes, who was considered a Rune master, how such people learned their craft and about the transmission of runic lore from master to apprentice.

What we do know is that the individual Runes took on sacred meanings and, with the passage of time, became the first abiding Oracle of Western Europe. Writing in 98 A.D., in Book X of his *Germania,* the Roman historian Tacitus provides us with the most often quoted and explicit description of Runes being used as an Oracle:

> They cut a branch from a fruit bearing tree and divided it into small pieces; these they mark with certain distinctive signs *(notae)* and scatter them at random and without order upon a white cloth. Then, the priest of the community . . . after invoking the gods and with eyes raised to heaven, picks up three pieces, one at a time, and interprets them by means of the signs previously marked upon them.*

---

*Ibid.

While Tacitus says no more concerning the nature of the *notae,* Professor Elliott comments: "Undoubtedly by his time they were runes."

From Russia to Orkney, From Greenland to Greece

The Runes were carried from place to place by traders, adventurers and warriors, and even by Anglo-Saxon missionaries. The runic glyphs served to record business transactions, to write poetry, compose sagas and to embellish buildings, swords and the prows of ships. Runic artifacts and inscriptions are found in the Orkneys, the Shetlands and mainland of Scotland, in Greece, Greenland and deep inside Russia. Runic inscriptions have also been found in North America, although as yet no scholar will agree that any such finds are genuine.

We learn a great deal from the inscriptions on *runstenar,* the monumental Rune stones found throughout Scandinavia. Placed as they often were at crossroads or river crossings, they provided travelers with information about the ways Vikings made their money, conducted themselves in battle and how they died. The imposing Rune stones were erected partly as memorials, but frequently also served the public and semi-legal purpose of registering a death, especially when it was the death far from home of someone rich or important— someone whose death was bound to leave matters of inheritance, debt and allegiance to be sorted out by the heirs. Often, because of their abiding interest, the heirs' names would be clearly stated and credited with having erected the memorial stone.

My favorite monument from the period is an eighteen-foot-tall stone cross, known as the Ruthwell Cross for the church where it still stands in Dumfriesshire, Scotland. The principal inscription, intended to enhance the biblical scenes depicted on the cross, is carved in Runes. The lines are from an Old English poem, *The Dream of the Rood:*

> *Christ was on the cross.*
> *Still, many came swiftly,*
> *Journeying from afar,*
> *Hurrying to the Prince.*
> *I beheld it all.*

The poem's author is unknown. The voice speaking in the poem is the wood of the Cross.

The Runes reached their widest audience between A.D. 800 to 1200, the era when the Vikings were masters of Europe. When the Viking age ended, the Runes began to disappear. Their use as an alphabetic script dwindled away. And the wisdom of the Rune masters died with them, for all that was sacred in their tradition was passed on verbally and never written down. Finally, in 1639, the use of Runes in Iceland was officially forbidden. For almost 350 years, the Runes were silent and the blessing of the Oracle was lost to us.*

Now, with a resurgence of desire for a closer relationship with the Divine, the oracular tradition will be understood for what it truly is and, in time, restored to its rightful place in the lives of God's people.

---

*For a fuller history of both the Runes and the oracular tradition, see *The Book of Runes.*

Navajo Song

The mountains,
I become part of it . . .
The herbs, the fir tree,
I become part of it . . .
The morning mists, the clouds,
The gathering waters,
I become part of it . . .
The wilderness, the dewdrops, the pollen,
I become part of it.

—Anonymous

In Praise of the Oracular

And the oracle he prepared in the house within, to set there the ark of the covenant of the Lord.

—I Kings 6:19

It is always there. Whenever we need an answer it is there. No matter what the situation, our higher self knows exactly what is best for us. It is not a political, social or intellectual self; it is the core of our being. No matter how long it's been since we consciously communicated with it, the power within us remains steady. . . . It works overtime all the time. It doesn't matter whether we went to church last Sunday or if we haven't been since whenever, if ever. The spirit within is there for us, always. We just have to acknowledge it, praise it, thank it and know everything is all right now.

—Iyanla Vanzant

So ancient are the Runes that their appearance, predating as it does the birth of Christ, qualifies them as the oldest truly Western Oracle we possess. From the beginning of recorded time, we have evidence of the prevalence and sacredness of Oracles. The word has its origin in the Latin *oraculum*, from *orare*, to speak or pray, and means, first and foremost, a

Divine message, a command or announcement from on High.

The word "Oracle" stands also for the mechanism or medium through which Divine communication arrives: tortoise shells heated in the fire until cracks appeared in them. Pictures found in clouds, in the flight of birds, on the surface of water. Words spoken from a whirlwind or from the fiery heart of a burning bush. Messages marked on bone, baked in clay and cut into stones. Messages from the Divine coming, it seems, from everywhere and anywhere for those with ears to hear and eyes to see.

The oracular tradition stretches around the globe: Oracle bones have been found in China; in Africa a variety of tribal peoples relied on the oracular for their wisdom and their survival. In 1986, when I met with Don Diego, the spiritual leader of the Yaqui Indians, and showed him the runic glyphs, he told me that his people also possessed their own Oracle. Then he took a stubby pencil and, on a piece of brown shopping-bag paper, drew seven of the letters from his people's own oracular script, each of which mirrored one of the Runes.

It is a fact: A significant number of diverse cultures have, in their time, possessed an oracular tradition by means of which to discover the will of the Divine for the lives of the people.

God's Fax Machines

Although a large part of the oracular tradition is lodged in ancient cultures, we are not as far distant from that tradition as you might think. The connection is found in what a friend of ours likes to call "home Oracles, God's Fax Machines."

There is a long history of these home Oracles, methods people have devised for consulting the Divine in private. The Healing Runes belong to this tradition.

In Roman times, using a technique known as *Sortae Vergiliane,* anyone seeking advice about what constituted right action in any situation would open Virgil's *Aeneid* and read the first line upon which their eyes fell. For centuries, here in the West, those wishing to learn the Will of the Divine on any matter have consulted the dictionary and the Bible in a similar manner.

The most popular American Oracle was known as "Noah Webster's Oracle." Members of our grandparents' generation, when they were stumped or puzzled or in need of advice, would open the dictionary at random, place their finger anywhere on the page and take counsel from the words their finger indicated.

Over the years, I have met people who, without any precise knowledge of Oracles or the oracular tradition, opened their Bibles in the same manner and with the same intention, and called upon the wisdom of Holy Writ to set a light at their feet and show them the path. In our own time, and in keeping with ancient oracular tradition, Holy Writ is still being consulted as a guide to right action and correct conduct.

There exists such a variety of oracular instruments. It has long been my habit to consult the *Daily Word** and live by its wisdom. Other people use Oracles of their own devising—however homespun—and receive wise counsel. It appears

---

*Daily Word is an excellent compilation of daily inspirational readings published, monthly, by Unity, Unity Village, MO 64065.

that as the pressure on our lives increases, we are witnessing a resurgence of the oracular tradition.

What is new is the magnitude of the phenomenon, and the wide commercial availability of oracular instruments—popular, affordable works of sacred art, such as *The Medicine Cards*[*] and the *Sacred Path Cards*.[†]

Listening to Your Heart

Few of us today recognize the power once conveyed by the word "Oracle." You might not know what to reply if someone asked you: "Have you ever had an oracular experience?" Let me put the question another way: Have you ever felt the presence of the Divine, or had God answer your prayers when you prayed? If the answer is yes, you have indeed experienced the oracular.

This book, however, is more a user's manual than a historical survey. The function of any Oracle is to help put you in touch with the part of yourself that knows everything you need to know for your life now. Using the Healing Runes is one way to talk to God, and to listen when God speaks.

One thing needs to be said before you even begin to work with the Oracle: With time and experience, you will find that you can put the Oracle aside and simply *know*.

We are embossed with the image of the Divine; in truth, we are the Oracle, quite capable of ascertaining all necessary

_____

[*]Jamie Sams and David Carson, *The Medicine Cards* (Santa Fe, NM: Bear & Co., 1988).
[†]Jamie Sams, *Sacred Path Cards* (San Francisco: HarperCollins, 1990).

wisdom from our meditations, from our prayer life with the Holy Spirit, from stillness itself. Psalm 46, verse 10, sets the conditions for oracular listening in one simple and perfect instruction: *Be still, and know that I am God.*

Do you remember Jiminy Cricket's straightforward advice in *Pinocchio* to "always let your conscience be your guide"? The truth is that, ultimately, we do not need anything external to speak to us of what is right. And when inner stillness is achieved, healing of some kind is most surely taking place.

Although the first steps of the healing journey were taken by the Chinese, masters of many pulses, in the West it was the Egyptians who discovered the human pulse and called it "the voice of the heart." Melody Beattie, in her book *The Lessons of Love*, writes: "To know the mind of God . . . listen to your heart."*

The pulse, the heart, the mind of God: the vital signs of the oracular.

---

*Melody Beattie, *The Lessons of Love* (New York: HarperCollins, 1994).

Nothing New

A Course in Miracles *and aikido say much the same thing: Forgive, do not fear, do not anticipate attack, focus all your energy in the here and now of your body and mind. Be at peace. Be still. And in the stillness and peace, let your seeing and your listening come from Total Self, which contains the unencumbered will of God. And in the free form of Creation, you will know the moves to make.*

—A Course in Miracles

Using the Healing Runes

Did you know that the very energy and vitality of God lie within you, just waiting to be called forth? You can claim your wholeness now by affirming with bold faith and conviction: The all-powerful life of God moves in and through me, and I am whole, well and strong. Thank You, God.

—*Daily Word*

Everything in life is apt to be very interesting when the sacred comes to call.

—Caroline Myss

How do the Healing Runes work? You are in crisis. It feels like your world is coming apart. You are facing a challenge and need the advice of a trusted friend. But your doctor, therapist and best friends are nowhere to be found. With your issue in mind, do the following:

One, pick a Rune. Reach into your bag and draw out one stone.

Two, look up the Rune's picture and page number inside the cover of this book.

Three, turn to the Interpretation and read the commentary

for that Rune to help you get in touch with your feelings in the present situation.

To be sure, not every sentence of an Interpretation will be relevant to each of you. Yet, each time you draw a Rune, there will always be a few key phrases that speak clearly to your needs and your concerns. On occasion, what's more, the Oracle will even override your present concern and point you toward another difficult situation, another area of your life, that is crying out for attention.

From the time I first began to consult the Oracle, back in the summer of 1977, it has always been my practice to think things through as far as I could by myself, or offer them up in prayer, before turning to the Runes. Sometimes, mind you, that process took only seconds. The point I'm making here is this: The Healing Runes are an invaluable tool to assist us when we meditate on our situations. But they are nothing more than a tool.

The truth of these Runes lies in their power to serve us on our healing journey. Whatever in your life calls out for healing, the Healing Runes will support you in making wise and loving decisions.

There are so many times when you will find the Oracle helpful in the course of daily living, though not necessarily on a daily basis. More likely, on a need-to-know basis. As you become familiar with this oracular instrument, you will know what to ask and when.

Each of you will go through different phases in your relationship to the Oracle as a self-counseling tool. There will be times when you use the Healing Runes daily, other times when you use them not at all. Like the Viking Runes before them, the Healing Runes are proving themselves to be a trustworthy witness and good companion for those who have chosen self-healing as their path. When you find yourself at a crossroads, in a life crisis or, simply, when you are faced with any question of right action, and you desire to act for the highest good of all concerned, the Oracle is there to serve you.

This Book Was Written for You

In recent years, Recovery has become a multibillion dollar American industry. Best-selling authors—among them, John Bradshaw, Melody Beattie, Robin Norwood, M. Scott Peck and Marianne Williamson—have sold in excess of 80 million books. There are countless cassette tapes, seminars and workshops. However, in all that is offered in the extensive healing market, there has been no hands-on tool people could turn to for immediate feedback and insight in moments of pain, fear, confusion and self-doubt. *The Healing Runes* is designed to support people, counsel them and strengthen their desire and resolve to heal in all phases of the Recovery process.

Susan and I developed *The Healing Runes* for:

○ People already in all forms of therapy and Recovery as well as those working the various Twelve Step programs.

○ The family members of the 100 million addicts whose lives are adversely affected on a daily basis.

○ The huge "undeclared" Recovery population. From teenagers to grandparents, those who suffer from the same isolation, fear, shame and grief as the millions in traditional Recovery, and yet are unable or unwilling to join a program or seek help.

○ Therapists; those involved in peer counseling; men's and women's groups and support groups of all kinds; those concerned with healing from the effects of disease (cancer, AIDS, terminal illnesses), gender issues and severe economic setbacks.

○ Teenagers who may never read a Recovery book, seek therapy or attend a Twelve Step Program, but who will "play a game" of reaching into a bag and pulling out a stone.

○ All those who seek to restore their conscious connection with God, and in so doing regain their physical, emotional and spiritual health.

The key to working effectively with the Healing Runes is always to begin with the personal and then extend healing to our families, our schools, out into the streets, into our communities and, eventually, throughout our nation and the world. Whether you are facing emotional problems, addictions, physical illness or relationship issues, the Runes have a purpose and a function in *any* situation where healing is called for.

The Healing Runes are a mirror that provides you with an immediate emotional and psychological reflection of where you are in your own Recovery, and then gently encourages you to move on, to take your Recovery out into the world and make a difference.

Calling on the Runes

The following are some times and situations when you might consult the Healing Runes for support and guidance. Particularly at the beginning, when I was still learning the Rune names and order, I tended to draw a Rune each morning when I got up. Sometimes I'd want to check on an issue, or know how someone else was getting along. But mostly, I just wanted a Rune-for-the-Day to give me a hint of what my unconscious considered timely. To coordinate my will with the Will of the Divine for my life this day. And to make me conscious of my opportunity to make an adjustment in my life's course and, hence, its destiny.

When It's Time to Take the Next Step

When you are ready to take a step, and you really need to talk things out; when you need a friend and there isn't one around at the moment; when you don't feel comfortable enough with the people around you to share what you are feeling: Open your bag of Runes. In it you will find a friend. The late David Susskind called the Runes "Dear Abby in a bag."

When There Are Issues of Health

If you are facing a challenge with your health, the Healing Runes can be both a companion for the journey and a source of good counsel. Ask for any further clarification about your condition that would help, and draw a Rune. But always remember and believe that each of us has the ability, from deep within, to heal our emotions, our bodies and our spirits.

Using the Runes supports our recognition and acceptance of our God-given healing power; power we can access through faith and prayer. More than ever, we are being forced back on our own resources. Universal health care begins right now, with each of us.

In Matters of the Heart

If you are facing a difficult conversation with a spouse or partner, you will be able to use the Oracle to check the emotional "weather" at the moment. Or you might use the Oracle to consider the psychological barriers to cooperation and union, emotional conditions that prevent negotiation and sabotage all efforts at resolving the conflict at hand.

Whether you are already in a new relationship, or considering entering one, let the Healing Runes assist you on your journey. Think of the person with whom you are concerned. Then draw a Rune, posing questions such as: "What must I be mindful of as I begin this new relationship?" Or you might ask: "What do I need to remember about myself in caring for this relationship?" You may receive the Rune of *Forgiveness* ᛗ or *Patience* ᛇ, in effect reminding yourself to practice those virtues. The Rune of *Boundaries* ᛦ may serve to make you especially mindful of personal boundaries as you begin a new relationship, lest you repeat the mistakes of the past. Then again, you might ask the Oracle: "What is there about this person that I need to understand more clearly?"

If you are already in a relationship, and the time for a decision is at hand, ask the Healing Runes for guidance and support. And trust that your heart will hear what you need to hear.

In Matters of Family

Within your own family, be it your birth family or your chosen family, there will come times of discord and disharmony. When those times arise, take the opportunity to restore harmony and balance by exploring your feelings about the situation. Ask for guidance and draw a Healing Rune.

Discord

Say there is a situation of what we call family discord, a sore subject someone will always touch upon through lack of sensitivity or, in certain families, just to stir things up. Pick a Rune for a new way to respond in that situation.

Abuse

For those of you either beginning to look at childhood abuse, or well along the way, use the Healing Runes as a friend who will listen: You will be reminded of what needs to be heard or said one more time. What is it I need to know to sustain me and give me courage? What is the next insight I require to continue my process of healing? Bear in mind that healing from all forms of abuse takes patience, understanding, acceptance, love and compassion.

When Someone Is Dying

With a dying parent, a friend, a lover, as you sit at the bedside, questions will come to you; matters you long to speak about; amends that need to be made while there is time. Even when the dying person cannot speak, we have always found the Runes to be profound and accurate interpreters for what needs to be said or understood. Make sure you take time to explore what you are feeling, and find new ways to express and share some of those feelings with those you love.

Relationships in the Workplace

Sometimes there will be conflicts that arise in our working relationships with our bosses, our co-workers or our employees that require some form of resolution or, at least, clarification. Here too, when you have exhausted your own ideas, the Healing Runes can be reliable sources of insight and wisdom. Let them aid you in calming the waters and support you in your desire to create a more productive work environment for everyone involved.

When You Know Something to Be True

You may feel certain that something is true even when those around you cannot see it. Or you may find yourself in a situation where you get a nagging feeling that something is not quite right. It is often difficult to put these feelings into words, to explain precisely what you mean.

These are times when we need confirmation for what we are feeling. Often, those feelings can only be shared with ourselves. In such moments, the Runes are a hand mirror of truth showing us reflections of love.

A country doctor I know was feeling overwhelmed by his practice, by the new techniques he needed to learn, the mass of literature to be read, the patient load he was handling by himself. One day, I jokingly suggested he make a run for it, turn over his practice and do a year in the Peace Corps. He really liked the idea and told me it "felt" right. But then, all the logical reasons not to do any such thing began to surface. "Stop," I said. "Pick a Rune."

"And ask what?"

"For the Oracle to comment on you and the Peace Corps." I held out my bag, he took it, felt around inside and came up with ⊠. I gave him the book, and he opened it to the eighth Rune, *Faith,* lip-read down the page, nodding. Then, pointing with his finger, he read aloud: "*Faith encourages us to believe that we can make a difference—a difference first in ourselves, and then in the world. It was Gandhi who said that we must* be *the change we wish to see in the world.*"

Six weeks later, I saw my doctor friend off to India.

As Part of Your Prayer Life

Some days, before I begin to pray, I will take a Rune from my bag and lay it in front of me, face down. Then I ask to be guided to deal with some issue I might avoid were it not for a reminder from the Runes. While writing this chapter, I did precisely that, and got ⋈, the Rune of *Forgiveness.* In the Interpretation, my eye was drawn to the words: "*Joy in forgiving, and joy at being forgiven, hang level in the balances of love.*" I scanned my life, and knew at once where I had withheld forgiveness—in this instance, from myself.

When You Have No Questions, No Issues

When you are feeling uncertain, and still you have no particular question to ask or issue to identify, here is a question I came upon long ago. It seems so simple, at first glance, yet time and again over the years, the Oracle's response has been illuminating. The question is this: *What do I need to consider for my life now?*

The Eleventh Step

For more than two years, Father James Kirschhoffer led a Twelve Step meeting in Marin County, California. Kirschhoffer, a psychotherapist and former Episcopal priest, used the Runes in the weekly meetings he facilitated. He called those meetings "The Eleventh Step," the objective being: "Through prayer and meditation, to improve our conscious contact with God." Most meetings have some sort of emphasis; this was Kirschhoffer's. We recently asked him about the Marin County meetings.

Why did he work with the Runes?

"Something miraculous takes place in these rooms, with the community. If, in fact, you understand that there is a Higher Power, the Runes are one manifestation, historically, of that Higher Power's workings. Something that has a cere-monial nature, a physical nature, I find helpful—the stones, the book, the bag. Reaching into oneself involves all parts of the body: the three ancient centers, belly, heart and head."

Was there conflict when he introduced the Runes at the meetings?

"At first, I experienced conflict from inside the Twelve Step community, yes. But that didn't stop us. The Runes are so helpful, so consistent. People just kept coming back."

How did it work?

"I designed the Rune work as the central piece of the Eleventh Step meetings. We went around the circle and every-one drew a Rune. Then, one by one, those who wanted to, reflected on the Rune they'd received in relation to their life during the past week. That became the most powerful part of the meeting. People were just blown away. And it happened every time. In Recovery, new food for thought is always required."

How does he account for the Runes' impact?

"The Runes are simply a parallel stream to the stream of spiritual energy. We know the Program works if you work it; if you do the Steps, you can be healed of your addictions. That's been demonstrated. Correspondingly, if you are open to the energy of the Runes, it comes from the same place. Just as the Twelve Step form is perfect for the community, so the Runes are eminently suitable for the community and, far more so, for the individual in the community. Again and again, I have been helped to identify my own lenses and filters, first through *The Book of Runes*, and now through *The Healing Runes*."

Over the years, we have received letters from people in a variety of Twelve Step programs describing ways in which the Runes contributed to their working the steps. As in any period of great change, there is always a pioneer. We are all most grateful to James Kirschhoffer for opening a door that was tightly closed.

Runic Override

Occasionally, you may find that the Rune you draw does not seem to apply to the issue you had in mind. When this occurs, consider the possibility that your unconscious has tuned in to a more relevant or pressing issue, something you may be avoiding, or of which you are not immediately aware. Runic

Override serves, in such moments, as an automatic fail-safe device. Similarly, when you find yourself considering two issues and are uncertain which one to address, draw a Rune anyway. The Oracle—which is to say your own Inner Knowing—will usually speak to the more pressing issue.

Conversations with the Oracle

There have been times, especially when I was driving long distances, that I found myself holding conversations with the Oracle. I would have an issue in mind and would draw a Rune. Considering that Rune's Interpretation would move me along in my thinking and, often, bring up another aspect of the situation. So I would take another Rune. Sometimes this practice might extend to seven or eight Runes and last for several hours, between thinking, drawing the next Rune, considering its Interpretation and keeping my eyes on the road. These "dialogues" are really two-way conversations that can be entertaining, informative and good for what ails you when you're feeling lonely.

Yes and No Answers

There is a basic courtesy that attaches to the Oracle. Primarily this consists in *not* asking questions that call for a yes or no answer. As a general rule, *the Runes do not provide answers*. To give someone the answer to significant questions robs them forever of acquiring the answer for themselves. "What steps do I need to take in this situation?" would be an appropriate question. "Should I leave this relationship?" would not. Instead, pose the question as an *issue,* asking the Oracle to comment on the advisability of leaving or not.

Having made this point, I want to offer an exception. There will come times when you find yourself in a situation where you are required to make an immediate decision. No time for reflection, to check things out or get more information. The telephone rings and someone says: "Will you or won't you? Yes or no?" When that occurs, I need a way to get myself off "stuck."

The answer is simple enough: I use two Runes— ⑤ and ①, which in their original meanings stood for *fire* (the sun) and *ice*—and let ⑤ stand for "Yes" and ① for "No."

Simply remember that this technique is not meant to be used when examining issues of substance. Yet it can be very helpful at moments when what you do or don't do matters less than getting on with your life.

Lending Your Runes

Lending your Runes to someone else is strictly a personal matter. Some people will feel comfortable lending their Runes, others will not. For me, the Runes are, first and last, a means of communication—with my Knowing Self and with God. I am always comfortable sharing my Runes, but then I am also content to lend my car and even my computer. If you are in doubt about lending your Runes, consult the Oracle.

Keeping a Healing Runes Journal

I can remember when I was a kid and still growing how, at the end of each summer, my father would have me stand with my head against the frame of my closet door and, with a thick wooden pencil, make a mark to show how much I had grown. We moved only three times during my childhood, but I liked to think of the next kid to have my bedroom finding those marks and their dates on the closet door frame.

As you begin to work with the Healing Runes, you may find it useful to record the Runes you draw and the insights that come from certain spreads. My habit has been to note the date and the prevailing conditions in my life at that moment. Recording your Rune readings will, in the beginning of your practice, serve to help you become more familiar with the essence of the individual Runes. Looking back, the journal will help you to recall with some accuracy where you were in a cycle or pattern. Finally, in the light of later events, you will be able to judge for yourself the relevance and accuracy of the Oracle as a guide for healing and self-change.

In addition, I used my Rune Journal to record curious coincidences involving Runes. Here are two items from my journal. One occurred several years ago, while I was rereading a novel I had written, published in 1973, in which the young hero describes his grandfather's writing as "a runic squiggle." If there's one thing Runes don't do, it's squiggle. Still, I took that reference as a single brush stroke that had prefigured an entire canvas, and noted it in my Rune Journal.

There is another journal entry made shortly after I began working with the Runes. I was reading *Timber Line—A Story of*

Bonfils and Tannen, by Gene Fowler.* What won the book a journal footnote was Fowler's description of the penmanship of an old *Denver Post* journalist, Joe Ward, who "wrote a hand which none but a student of cave-dweller runes might decipher." And why not? By extended definition the word "rune" came to include any of the "scratches" our early ancestors used to signify meaning. Just another growth mark on the frame of time's closet door.

Ancient as they are, the Runes remain an open-ended system. In time, you will no doubt discover new and creative ways to enjoy and benefit from them.

I think often of Dr. Wallace K. Reid's comment that "the oracular *is* scriptural." Those words lit up the entire landscape for me and helped me to realize that the oracular must not be regarded by Christians as a minefield. Only the stern huntsmen of orthodoxy attempt to ride us with blinders, short reins and a martingale. The Divine requires us to be free.

---

*Gene Fowler, *Timber Line—A Story of Bonfils and Tannen* (New York: Covici Friede, 1933).

Reflections on Death

When you love, give it everything you've got
And when you have reached your limit—
  give it more.
And forget the pain of it,
  because as you face your death
  it is only the love you have given
  and received that will count.
And all the rest—
  the accomplishments, the struggles, the fights—
  will be forgotten in your reflections.
If you have loved well
  then it will have been worth it.
The joy of it will last through the end;
  but if you have not,
  death will always come too soon. . . .

—Elisabeth Kübler-Ross

Healing Rune Spreads

Breathing in, I calm body and mind.
Breathing out, I smile.
Dwelling in the present moment.
This is the only moment.
Present moment.
Perfect moment.

—Thich Nhat Hanh

When we cannot be real and creative, we cannot discover, explore and complete our stories and thereby grow and develop. We cannot have peace.

—Charles Whitfield, M.D.

Over the years, I have developed a set of basic techniques for accessing the Runes. Certain of these techniques or spreads were based upon ancient patterns, others were freshly minted. A considerable number of people have shared with me their responses to the spreads. Others have provided ideas for new techniques. As you work with the Healing Runes, and new ideas for helpful spreads come to you, if you have your own favorite ways of accessing the Will of the Divine, please share them with us.

The Rune of Guidance

Technically, a single Rune is not a spread. And yet, if one glance at the compass tells you how to modify your course setting, what more is required?

This is the most practical and simple use of the Oracle, and consists of drawing one Rune for an overview of an entire situation. This can assist you to focus more clearly on your issue and provide you with a fresh perspective. What you are in effect doing is inviting the mind to function intuitively, and invoking the wisdom of the Knowing Self.

At any time, in any situation, when you feel the need to listen to the wisdom of your Higher Self, or your Higher Power, a single Rune drawn from the bag will serve you like a glimpse of a compass, in order to reassure you about the course you are taking.

Drawing a single Rune is particularly helpful under stressful conditions. You may find yourself dealing with matters that demand action now, and the truth is, *you don't have enough information.* To reach a decision, all you require is your bag of Runes and, if possible, a quiet place.

Drawing a single Rune is not valuable only in a time of crisis; this technique is useful whenever you require an overview of any situation. Remember, you can always pick a Rune as a reality check. Once a week, once a month, every day. You'll know when.

On a long drive or commute between home and work, some people keep their Runes beside them on the seat. Drawing the Rune of Guidance often reveals the humor in a difficult matter. And why not? God's favorite music is said to be laughter.

If you are concerned about someone who is far away and you are unable to contact that person, focus directly on the individual, and then draw a Rune. This practice opens a doorway in the mind to the non-ordinary. You may find that it is, indeed, possible to know things at a distance, and that your true vision extends as far as the mind and heart can see.

Use the single Rune drawing to honor significant events in your life: birthdays, anniversaries, the New Year, even the death of a friend and other important occasions. You may want to record these readings in a Rune Journal.

Three Healing Runes

The number "three" figures prominently in the oracular traditions of the ancients. Drawing three Runes (a practice which was already in use two thousand years ago according to the Roman historian, Tacitus) is satisfactory for all but the most demanding situations.

With an issue clearly in mind, select three Runes, one at a time, and place them in front of you in order of selection, from left to right. You may want to lay them face down and then turn them over.

Once you have selected the Runes, they will lie before you in this fashion: The Runes represent *Body* on the left; *Mind* in the center; and *Spirit* on the right.

Body	*Mind*	*Spirit*
1	2	3

Here are some questions you might ask yourself as you consider the Interpretations for the Runes in this spread.

Body

If you are being physically challenged, you may want to consider what is going on in the present situation. Can you recall some of the events in your life that may have contributed to what your physical body is now facing? Take care that you do not find fault with *how* you got where you are. Illness can be a great gift, providing us, as it does, with the opportunity to focus on ourselves and our lives. In prayer or meditation, take a moment for thoughts or insights on what might be your first step on the healing path.

Mind

What are you thinking and feeling? What is your head saying? Is your mind overriding what you are feeling? Are you listening to your body and to your feelings, or are you listening only to your head?

Spirit

Are you being mindful of the care of your soul? Are you doing the work necessary to nourish your soul? What condition is your spirit in? Can other people see it? Is your spirit broken; if so, what can you do to mend it so it can continue to do God's work?

A Sample Reading

If you find yourself dealing with a childhood wound, you might ask: "What do I need to do for myself today to continue on my healing journey?" Say that the Runes you draw are *Anger* Ⓝ, *Surrender* Ⓡ and *Trust* Ⓧ. The spread would look like this:

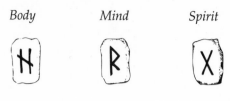

Body   *Mind*   *Spirit*

19. Anger   20. Surrender   · 2. Trust

Begin with Body. Take time to explore the reasons you are feeling angry about the situation at hand. Now turn to the Rune of *Anger*. You might find the relevant lines from the Interpretation to be: "*See if you can find a safe passage that leads from the present situation to a place of harmony and peace?*" Next, if it is within your power, identify the changes you need to make to ease your anger, thereby freeing yourself to move on to the next stage, which is one of surrender.

If you have sufficient time, leave a few minutes after reading each interpretation before moving on to the next one. Use that time, perhaps, to meditate on the words you read.

Now, consider the position of Mind. Receiving the Rune of *Surrender,* you are being asked to relinquish your control in the current situation, thereby acknowledging your readiness to heal. The voice speaks of the willingness to change. In the Interpretation, you might focus on: "*If you are facing a critical illness, a life crisis, or if the moment has finally come to stop fighting yourself, be grateful, and practice surrender.*"

In the place of Spirit, you are being asked to show trust, either in this present situation—however difficult or painful it may be—or in preparing for what lies ahead. Words from the Interpretation to comfort and sustain you in your present situation might be these: "*However oppressive or painful the moment may seem, this Rune urges you to have faith and to know that, as you heal, you* will *be able to trust again."* These words speak for the Spirit.

Five Healing Runes

More often than not, drawing a single Rune—the Rune of Guidance—will provide you with sufficient information and insight to enable you to determine what is appropriate in any situation. However, there will be times when your need to know far outruns the scope of a single Rune stone, or even a Three Healing Runes spread. The *Five Healing Runes* can help you to identify the distinctive features of a situation that might otherwise threaten to overwhelm you with its complexity.

Begin by clearly formulating your issue. Next, draw five stones from the bag, one at a time, and lay them out one below the other. In descending order, let the Runes stand for the following:

1. *Heart in the Past (Overview)*

2. *Heart in the Present (Challenge)*

3. *Appropriate Action*

4. *Obstacle (Surrender)*

5. *New Situation (Opportunity)*

1. Heart in the Past (Overview)
   This is the overview of where you have been in the past, emotionally or spiritually, with regard to the situation at hand.

2. Heart in the Present (Challenge)

This Rune will aid you in hearing what your heart is trying to tell you. It offers an opportunity to explore your own insights and, at the same time, stay present with what you are feeling.

3. Appropriate Action

First of all, is there something you need to do for yourself in order to take the next step? Second, are you mindful of any considerations that will assure right action in this situation?

4. Obstacle (Surrender)

This is about believing in yourself by surrendering into the present situation. Someone has said that you must clear out your mind before you put in the truth. Surrender as a mark of self-esteem, as evidence that you trust yourself and your feelings.

5. New Situation (Opportunity)

This Rune will afford you a new and clearer view of the situation that results from taking appropriate action. Use this opportunity to apply the skills you have learned on your healing journey.

A Sample Reading

Given the time in which we live and the increasing pressures we all must endure, here is a question that opens out in many directions: *What is it in myself that has kept me from seeing my life more clearly?*

These are the Runes I drew:

 1. Heart in the Past (Overview)

 2. Heart in the Present (Challenge)

 3. Appropriate Action

 4. Obstacle (Surrender)

 5. New Situation (Opportunity)

Below is a brief commentary for each of the Runes, followed by a few lines from the Rune's Interpretation:

1. Heart in the Past (Overview): Denial

Denial is like a chameleon, constantly changing, according to our needs and fears. Facing and breaking through our Denial requires enormous effort, diligence and honesty.

Interpretation: *"It counsels you to open yourself up and let the Light into a part of your life that has been secret, shut away."*

2. Heart in the Present (Challenge): Boundaries

To reclaim your life, or to gain control or understanding in your present situation, take the time now to establish appropriate Boundaries. Both internal and external. If you have not yet learned how to set appropriate Boundaries, don't be hard on yourself. Ask for guidance and strength and try again. In time, you will learn.

Interpretation: *"In the Circle of the Runes, healthy Boundaries always bear witness to the fact that someone has courageously undertaken the journey from Denial to Honesty."*

3. Appropriate Action: ⓕ Honesty

At the heart of any situation, especially where our ability to heal is concerned, there is the opportunity for Honesty. Seize this opportunity, for without it true healing is impossible.

Interpretation: *"You are reminded that there is less of everything—less hope, less trust, less faith, less to life itself—without rigorous Honesty."*

4. Obstacle (Surrender): ⓑ Prayer

If you are feeling overwhelmed by the situation, there is only one thing to do: Ask for God's help through Prayer. Here you are encouraged to engage in whatever form of Prayer or meditation is soothing and healing for your saddened heart or spirit. Prayer reminds us that through faith, all things are possible.

Interpretation: *"The proper prelude to all things is Prayer, for it is through Prayer that we practice the Presence of God in our lives."*

5. New Situation (Opportunity): ⓜ Forgiveness

With this Rune, you are being asked to look to your past and examine an old hurt. To decide for yourself if today is the day to let that hurt go in Forgiveness. And if this idea feels too overwhelming, do what you can, step by step, day by day.

In the end, healing is still possible, but always more difficult to achieve without Forgiveness.

Interpretation: *"It has been said that to cling to resentment is to harbor a thief in your heart. For resentment robs you of your energy, your strength, your peace of mind and, ultimately, your ability to heal."*

The Rune of Summary

You may see fit to draw one more stone, a *Rune of Summary*, a single Rune to describe, in one statement, the essence of the other five Runes. To do this, you would replace all the Runes in the bag and then draw one Rune.

When I did, I got that the essence of ᚾ, ᛃ, ᚠ, ᛒ and ᛗ is ᚲ, the Rune of *Acceptance*. Turn to the fourteenth Rune and see for yourself how it embraces the other five meanings.

Moreover, in the order of the Runes, *Acceptance* is preceded by *Patience*, which certainly makes sense, for in my experience, true acceptance always requires more time than I'd have expected. And once *Acceptance* is in place, what it brings is *Courage*, which is comforting to know ahead of time.

In dealing with the Rune of Summary, you may find it helpful to create a question to explore the next level of Summary. In this case, the question might be: *What is it in myself that continues to keep me from seeing my life clearly?* Each Rune of Summary—in fact, each situation—will suggest useful questions. You may want to record such questions, and the pertinent parts of the reading that come in response, in your Rune Journal.

Rune Play

Do you remember, as a child, sitting in the dentist's office, feeling a little afraid? Do you remember how happy it made you when you found a coloring book with drawings of a dense, leafy jungle, and the caption: "How many monkeys can you find hidden in the jungle?" And when you looked really hard at the picture, there they were: monkeys outlined in tree bark, monkeys disguised as vines, monkeys made from the outlines formed between leaves, trunk monkeys, branch monkeys, root monkeys!

Early on when I began working with the Runes, I realized how frequently they appear in nature's forms: in tree branches, rock formations, clouds, in ripples on water. Even today, just when I am about to jump to critical conclusions about someone's behavior, a cloud, combed by the wind, stretches itself into the soft lightning-bolt form of ⟨, the Rune of *Compassion*.

Once you begin *Rune Play*, you will discover runic signs or glyphs not only in nature but on license plates and bridge scaffoldings, among graffiti on walls, in cracks in the pavement, in house beams and on road signs. When you really look, you will find Runes everywhere.

Say you draw a Rune in the morning. See if you can find the *same* runic symbol in the twisting branches of a favorite tree. During a meditation or while resting, visualize the Rune you picked, and hold it in your mind's eye. Stand in front of a mirror and form the glyph with your body—a kind of Rune yoga. Find the Rune in textures and on patterned surfaces. Finally, try to make that Rune the last image you see as you drift off to sleep at night.

Adventures in the Tunnel of Light

Among people who have reported near-death experiences, there are those who tell of another reality so beautiful that they actually felt anger at having to return to the world of the living. In *Embraced by the Light*,* Betty Eadie recounts how sometimes people spend the rest of their lives yearning for the amazing love and peace they found during their near-death experience. Others, on their return, feel cleansed and renewed, able to bring what they experienced into their daily life, and so to feel more fully the joy of each moment.

The goal is to learn to live life more fully. Take a moment and consider this: Have you ever thought what it would feel like to be facing the end of your life? Imagine that the moment has come for you to die. And yet there remains enough time for you to review your life and consider what you've left unfinished or incomplete. Words you wanted to say to someone but never said. Old relationships that went awry, where you would now gladly make amends. Aspects of your own nature that stand in need of transformation.

Take a moment to be still. Focus on your breathing; be aware of how precious each breath has become. Let all thoughts of the daily round depart; they are of no consequence to you now.

As you do this, consider the way you have lived your life, and choose one of the following questions. Then take a few moments and work with it:

---

*Betty Jean Eadie, with Curtis Taylor, *Embraced by the Light* (Placerville, CA: Gold Leaf Books, 1994).

○ What part of my life has been the most difficult for me?

○ What do I do best?

○ What or whom have I loved most?

○ With whom do I still have unfinished business?

○ What area of my life still calls for completion?

After you have decided on a question, choose a Rune and read the commentary. Then, if you still need more information, draw a second Rune. Other questions may occur to you; allow yourself to follow where they lead you.

Next, put your hand into the bag of stones and mix them, consciously touching each of them. Feel the blessings there and, with a lighter heart, review the progress you have made in widening your perspective and deepening your understanding.

Coping with Grief

Death and its attendant grief come to us all in time. Think back to your childhood and remember, if you can, the feelings you had when you first experienced a death. For many of you, it may have been when you lost a beloved pet. And for some of you, it may have been the greatest loss a child can suffer—the death of a parent.

What was it that helped you cope with that powerful experience of grief? Stay with the memory for a moment.

Then draw a Rune to help guide you through whatever form of "death" you are facing now, be it emotional, spiritual or physical. Consider what, in the Interpretation, best illuminates your situation. Usually people find that one special phrase or sentence speaks to you; ordinarily, that is enough.

For those of you who are now at the end of your own life's passage, may the blessings of heaven attend you. Our prayers go with you.

Finally, as part of your meditation, we ask you to include the people throughout the world whose hearts, whose families and whose countries are suffering. We ask you to pray for the men, women and children whose lives have been affected by cancer and by AIDS. We ask you to join us in daily prayers for their healing.

Prayer for Forgiveness

*All that we ought to have thought and have not
   thought,
All that we ought to have said and have not said,
All that we ought to have done and have not done,
All that we ought not to have thought and yet
   have thought,
All that we ought not to have spoken and yet have
   spoken,
All that we ought not to have done and yet have done,
For thoughts, words and works, pray we, O God,
   for forgiveness,
And repent with penance.
Amen.*

—Ascribed to Zoroaster
(c. 628–c. 551 B.C.)

A Circle of Healing Runes

Quench not the Spirit. Despise not prophesying. Prove all things; hold fast that which is good.

—I Thessalonians 5:19–21

It's what we all wanted when we were children—to be loved and accepted exactly as we were then, not when we got taller or thinner or prettier . . . and we still want it . . . but we aren't going to get it from other people until we can get it from ourselves.

—Louise Hay

True healing is found in the memory of wholeness.

—Deepak Chopra

A Circle of the Healing Runes is like a round of yoga postures practiced by a master: Each evolves from each, supported by the one that went before, and itself affording a foundation for the Rune that is to follow.

We begin in Innocence. Entering the Circle now, at any point, we proceed around the wheel, being healed and made whole on the journey of our return to Innocence.

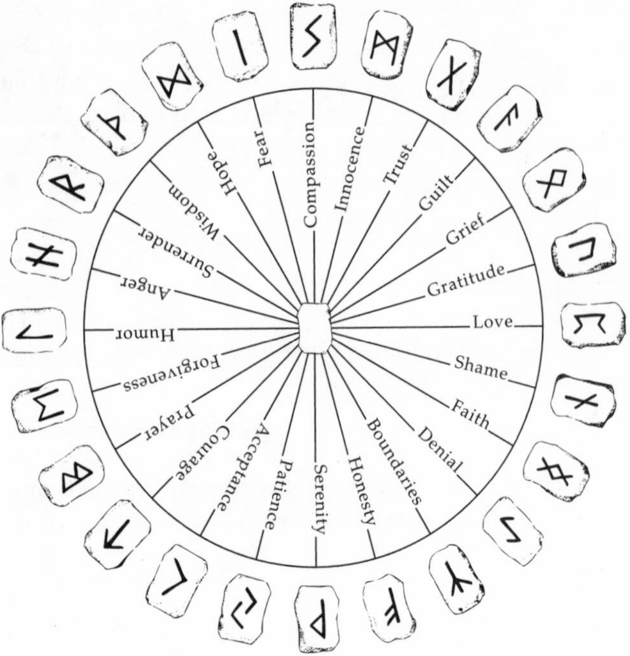

A Circle of Healing Runes

Let it be said this way:

The true beginning for each one of us lies in *Innocence*, and Innocence is recognizable in our willingness to *Trust*. As we begin to heal, let Trust prepare and strengthen us to face *Guilt* openly, and to embrace *Grief* with understanding. Seeing our progress, we grow in our capacity to feel *Gratitude*, which is among the first real signs of Love. There simply is no greater healing force than *Love*, Love that, by its very presence, dissolves *Shame*, and welcomes into our lives the light of *Faith*.

For when we see and live by Faith, it becomes less painful to dissolve *Denial* ⓘ and acknowledge the chaos Denial causes in our lives. From the sacred chemistry of Love and Faith arises the desire to honor one another, and to honor our true selves, by creating and maintaining solid *Boundaries* ⓨ. As we learn to recognize these Boundaries, *Honesty* ⓟ makes a trustworthy surveyor. Honesty-in-action prepares the ground both for *Serenity* ⓟ, and for Serenity's life partner, *Patience* ⓧ. That which is appropriate to our lives always comes to us in God's good time. Know, therefore, that Patience, supported by Honesty and strengthened by Serenity, prepares the ground for *Acceptance* ⓚ and tempers the tools for a life lived with *Courage* ⓣ. To help us remember that Courage is both our birthright and our daily bread, *Prayer* ⓑ spreads its wide wings over all of our endeavors.

Whoever stands in the way of Prayer will come to know *Forgiveness* ⓜ, and in forgiving, contemplate anew the wild, creative *Humor* ⓘ of God's ways. And so it is that *Anger* ⓝ, soothed by Prayer, healed through Forgiveness, and viewed through Humor's eyes, cannot hold us hostage very long. Now, at last, we come to understand the freedom that is born out of *Surrender* ⓡ. How else could so much healing be vouchsafed us, each and every one? As our hearts are opened wider through Surrender, *Wisdom* ⓟ deepens everything we know. Now, at our side, stands Wisdom's ally, *Hope* ⓜ. Strengthened as we are by Hope and Wisdom, when we come to face our *Fear* ⓘ, we meet and overcome it with *Compassion* ⓢ, and thus regain what we had perhaps never lost, but only been denied: our *Innocence* ⓜ.

At the heart of the Circle of the Healing Runes stands *The Divine* ◯. With each Rune we draw, we come to recognize the healing imprint of the Divine Presence upon each moment of our lives. We join in circles from the time we first listen to campfire stories until the last days, when our dear ones circle around us to bring love and protection at our departing. The Divine is the fire at the center of all Circles.

Compass Points

My friend James Coburn calls the Runes "a compass for conduct." How apt the term is. Think of it: a compass to support and guide us in doing whatever contributes to our healing at every moment. Still, this is an unusual sort of compass, in that you can only get from one point, or one Rune, to another (whether side by side or many degrees apart) by way of the center, the focus of all circles, *The Divine*.

"Side by side" means something different here. In God, all things are side by side, and the Divine is always present—as is the case whenever two or more are gathered together in the Holy Name. As you make your way around the Compass of your day, the Oracle is saying, God is the only road to your next destination.

Whereas, in most situations, one Rune is enough to indicate what constitutes right action, drawing a single Rune does not require that you cross the Circle by way of *The Divine*. Nevertheless, from its position at the center of the compass, the Divine radiates and shines upon you. Always.

"Bracketing"

When I was a Cub Scout as a kid in California, World War II had just ended, and my dad bought me an army surplus compass. The metal was all camouflaged in jungle greens and browns, and the needle had to be released to spin freely. Unlocking my compass, watching the needle seek and then home in on North, always gave me a thrill. At the time, I couldn't have said why. Just that I loved to watch the needle seek and settle—the way the needle swung past North on either side, bracketing the target, then achieving a lock, swinging, bracketing and locking on. It wasn't till years later, hearing naval friends talk about "bracketing," the technique used for aiming at a target at sea, that I got it.

Think of picking a Rune as the swinging needle. The Rune you pick points in the direction of this present moment in your life.

The Four Directions

Consider, for a moment, the Runes that occupy the four cardinal points of the compass: *Compassion* in the North, *Serenity* in the South, *Love* in the East and *Humor* in the West.

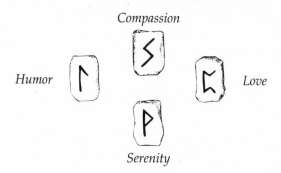

Compassion

Humor

Love

Serenity

This exercise in orientation may prove itself useful in the most diverse situations: A life that has temporarily broken down, or stalled, can be gotten back on the road with just these four Runes.

Exercise

Remove the four Runes and the Rune of *The Divine* from your bag and set the rest of the bag aside. Keeping *The Divine* to one side for now, place the four, face down, in front of you, moving them around until you no longer know which Rune is which.

Four Runes Turned Face Down   *The Divine*

Next, consider your issue. Perhaps it relates to a family split that has persisted because, until now, no one has taken the first step toward reconciliation. You might ask: "What does the Divine ask of me in this situation?"

Now turn up two of the four Runes. Say you get *Love* Ⓚ and *Humor* Ⓟ. Place one on each side of *The Divine* to represent the two aspects of *The Divine* most relevant in this situation. The spread will look like this:

Love   *The Divine*   *Humor*

Select two more Runes from those remaining in your bag. This time, let us say, you draw *Prayer* Ⓑ and *Patience* Ⓒ. Place the first Rune drawn above *The Divine* and the second below. Let the Rune above, *Prayer* ⚡, represent the response to the question: "How can I facilitate this process?" and let the Rune below, *Patience* ⟨⟩, be the response to the question: "What must I be mindful of that would make this healing possible?"

You now have the following layout:

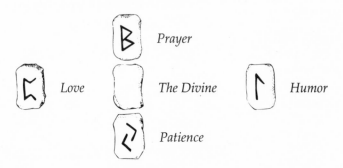

In brief, this pattern serves to remind you that *Love* can best be restored by moving slowly and gently, and by finding and sharing the *Humor* in this situation. You can help bring about the reconciliation, the Oracle is saying, by praying and by turning the outcome over to God. And then you must be patient, allowing whatever will happen to happen in God's good time.

While this spread is quite simple and brief to lay out, it usually suggests a fresh perspective on whatever challenges you.

Pairs

For this exercise, you might want to have two sets of Runes available. If not, copy the twenty-four glyphs onto pieces of cardboard and lay them out, in order, according to the sequence of Healing Runes (see page 56). The blank Rune is placed in the center.

Now, take your second set of Runes and, after setting the blank stone aside, take the Runes from your bag and place them—one by one, and without looking at the glyph before you do—facedown, to make a pair with the other twenty-four.

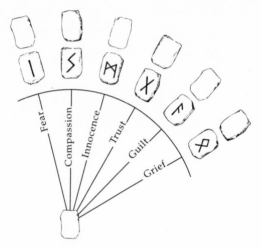

You now have an *Inner Circle* (the runic order) and an *Outer Circle* (the Runes as you drew them from the bag). As you turn each of the Runes in the Outer Circle faceup, you can consider it together with its paired Rune from the Inner Circle to discover how the combined Interpretations apply to your life.

The first few times I used this technique, I roared around the Circle, turning up Rune after Rune, until I had much too much to think about. The variety of combinations with Pairs is almost endless, different every time, and always, I find, relevant.

Since I use this Pairs layout quite often, it finally occurred to me how to simplify it: I turn up only one Rune, and take my bearings from that. Then, if I require further clarification, I turn over another.

On one occasion, I was in a situation where I simply would not allow someone to be who they were. I fought it. I resented it. I knew better what was good for them. My question was: "What keeps me from accepting them as they are, for what they are?" I turned up the Rune from the Outer Circle that was paired in the Inner Circle with *Acceptance* ⟨, and I found it was *Compassion* ⟩. Next—after asking: "What is keeping me from showing Compassion in this situation?"—I moved to *Compassion* on the Inner Circle, turned up the Rune paired with it and found *Fear* ⌷.

The message was direct and clear: *In order for you to show compassion and allow that person to be where they are—because that's where they are, and it's all right for them to be where they are—you must find quiet in yourself, and that cannot happen when you are afraid.*

A Daily Weather Report

Living our lives one day at a time, every day is a cycle and there is an emotional weather report for each day. Say that, upon waking, you draw a Rune and get *Anger*. Behind you lies *Humor*. Ahead waits *Surrender*. And across the Circle is *Shame*.

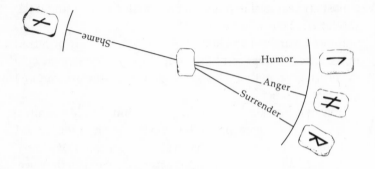

If you allow this section of the Circle to reflect the emotional weather for your day, it might help to remind you, when something arouses your anger, to call upon your sense of humor, your sense of the ridiculous. Surrender your will in the situation to the Divine; turn over to your Higher Power the outcome both for yourself and for others. Know that by exercising humor and surrendering when anger claims you, you will be spared all sense of shame.

A healing thought on a difficult and challenging day.

The Wheel of Hours

Consider each new day a journey through unfamiliar country. In the Healing Runes you have a trustworthy compass to confirm the direction in which you are traveling. Every so often, you can check to see where the needle points. But first, you must calibrate your compass to your day.

To begin with, we are counting the hours from 1 to 24, in the European manner. The true North position is hour No. 24, the position to its right is No. 1, then 2, and on around back to 24. That is to say, the first hour of the day is from midnight to 1:00; 1:00 to 2:00 is the second hour; 2:00 to 3:00 is the third hour; and on around to 11:00 P.M. to midnight as the twenty-fourth hour.

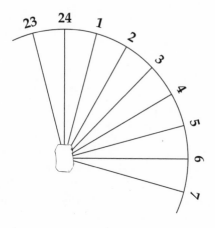

Sometime during your day, pick a Rune and note the time. The Rune you've chosen governs that hour of your day. Now rotate the Wheel so that the Runes are in the appropriate numbered-hour positions.

Let's try it out. For example, today, on waking, select a Rune and note the time. Let us say it is 6:30 A.M. and you chose the Rune of *Surrender* Ⓡ. If the first hour of the day is from midnight to 1:00, and the second from 1:00 to 2:00, then this Rune, *Surrender*, governs the seventh hour, which is from 6:00 to 7:00.

Now rotate the Wheel so that *Surrender* is in the seventh place and *Patience* Ⓧ, in the twenty-fourth or the midnight place, becomes the true North for this day. What you have now should look like the spread on page 66.

Begin your day with a meditation on *Surrender.* Read its Interpretation and consider what is occurring in your life where Surrender is an issue.

Lock the Wheel of Hours in place, then use it to take your bearings.

Now, suppose that around 3:40 in the afternoon, during the sixteenth hour of the day, you undergo a drop in the energy and drive you need to complete your work. Consider once more the Wheel of Hours. You will find that the hour from 3:00 P.M. to 4:00 P.M. (the sixteenth hour) is governed by *Gratitude* ⋂. Consider that Rune's application to the moment. Are you showing your gratitude to others on whom you rely? Are you feeling gratitude for what you have achieved during these past hours? Is this the moment to pause for a short time, to attend to your own needs, as a way of thanking yourself?

By now you can see how it works: Once your day has been set, remember the flow from one Rune to another ("Each evolves from each, supported by the one that went before, and itself affording a foundation for the Rune that is to follow"). The Runes keep their order, and they revolve, like a daily wheel of fortune that you spin once a day. Then you can take readings from any hour during which you might need clarification. Whether you use it or not, the information is there for you to draw upon.

Here's another example. Let's say that the first Rune you pick is after work, in the evening. It's been a difficult day: bad lunch, bad office conditions, arguments with friends or associates. It's 7:00 when you get home and draw a Rune. You get *Grief* ⊗. That figures.

First, meditate on the present, where you are now. What you have to be grateful for in your life, your friendships, children, the good air you breathe. Rotate the Wheel into position, then look back over your day, make a survey. Perhaps you can review the difficult lunch hour. Look to the Rune governing that hour. Since Grief is the nineteenth hour, count back to the hour between noon and 1:00 P.M., or the thirteenth hour, which is *Hope* ⋈. Turn to the Rune of Hope for what can be salvaged from the unfortunate lunch, and then move on.

After such a day, before you go to bed—say it's 10:40—consider the Rune that governs that hour, which is *Faith* ⊗. Review your entire day through the eyes of Faith.

Faith in action is the willingness to deal with life in the sure and certain knowledge that you will learn from your experience, overcome adversity and be healed.

At the very least, checking your Wheel of Hours from time to time during the day keeps you in the present, calls you to look up from what surrounds you, and lets you see the

broader perspective for your day, for your life. As my friend
Jim Kirschhoffer likes to say: "There is always only now."

The Function of *The Divine*

The Rune of *The Divine* is no longer simply the final glyph of a
twenty-five-letter alphabet. In the Circle of the Healing Runes,
it occupies its true station at the center of all things and the
heart of all matters. This is the message carved over the gate
of the Oracle: *No thing truly connects to any other thing except
through the Divine.*

And what about those moments when you draw a single
Rune, and the Rune you receive is *The Divine?* However else
you may interpret *The Divine,* take a moment to consider that
you are *at* the Center, and part *of* the Center, and choosing the
twenty-fifth Rune will always serve as a reminder of that.

Each time we take action in support of our healing, we
confirm the truth that *being responsible for our own lives is what
makes us human and enables us to grow closer to the Divine.*

As you wander around the Circle, you will begin to understand more about the invisible weaving of the Divine in our
lives, and to identify elements of the architecture that forms
the firm foundation for the Oracle.

Moreover, you will quickly come to recognize how easily
and gracefully any of these exercises may be modified to suit
the person using the Oracle. Many of you will no doubt, in
time, create your own variations; we hope you will share
them with us. In truth, there is no limit to the number of patterns such a Circle can encompass and contain.

Born to Manifest the Glory

Our deepest fear is not that we are inadequate.
Our deepest fear is that we are powerful beyond
  measure.
It is our light, not our darkness, that most frightens
  us.
We ask ourselves
  who am I to be brilliant, gorgeous, talented and
  fabulous?
Actually, who are you not to be?
You are a child of God.
Your playing small doesn't serve the world.
There is nothing enlightened about shrinking so that
  other people won't feel insecure around you.
We are born to make manifest the glory of God
  that is within us.
It's not just in some of us; it's in everyone.
And as we let our own light shine, we unconsciously
  give other people permission to do the same.
As we are liberated from our own fear,
  our presence automatically liberates others.

—Nelson Mandela
1994 Inaugural Speech

Rune Interpretations

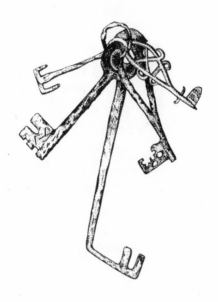

1. ᛗ Innocence, *73*
2. ᚷ Trust, *75*
3. ᚨ Guilt, *77*
4. ᚱ Grief, *79*
5. ᚾ Gratitude, *81*
6. ᚲ Love, *83*
7. ᛁ Shame, *85*
8. ᚷ Faith, *87*
9. ᛃ Denial, *89*
10. ᛉ Boundaries, *91*
11. ᚠ Honesty, *93*
12. ᚹ Serenity, *95*
13. ᛇ Patience, *97*
14. ᚲ Acceptance, *99*
15. ᛏ Courage, *101*
16. ᛒ Prayer, *103*
17. ᛗ Forgiveness, *105*
18. ᚦ Humor, *107*
19. ᚺ Anger, *109*
20. ᚱ Surrender, *111*
21. ᚦ Wisdom, *113*
22. ᛜ Hope, *115*
23. ᛁ Fear, *117*
24. ᛊ Compassion, *119*
25. ◻ The Divine, *121*

1. Innocence

The starting point is always Innocence. This Rune serves as a gentle reminder of the wholeness and simplicity we knew at our beginnings, and as a promise that we are finally coming home. For Innocence is our first nature, and from it flow all possible right relationships—with ourselves, with others and with the Divine.

The Rune of Innocence often marks a turning in the road: a cycle may be ending, a circle drawing to its close. At such a time, you are encouraged to remember the feelings of gentler days.

So many different things can bring back the sweet feelings of Innocence: a compassionate word, a smile, an act of kindness, all of which remind us of a time when life itself was effortless, a time when no one hurt our feelings, and the loving way we treated one another was the foundation of our existence. The very memory of those sweet feelings can be healing.

For those who have experienced the betrayal of Innocence, this Rune is saying: Be grateful both for your survival and for the wisdom you have gained through the pain and sorrow of the past. Ask God to once again place Innocence in your heart.

Receiving this Rune acknowledges the long road you have

traveled to arrive where you are today. Remember to honor yourself and those who have guided you. Allow yourself to feel, once again, the joy of Innocence, and know that you are being healed. For it is through healing that we reclaim our lost Innocence.

If you cut the Rune of Innocence in half, you will see the Rune of Serenity with its mirror image. There is a promise here, and a blessing. For when Serenity gazes into the mirror and recognizes its own likeness, it knows the peace and understanding that come with self-acceptance.

Use this day to simplify your life. Bring harmony where you find discord and balance where there is none. Take a moment for a prayer of remembrance and thanksgiving, a prayer offered up in childlike Innocence.

Let the Innocence you are feeling speak to the Innocence in everyone you meet.

2. Trust X

This is a Rune of restoration. It calls for the rebuilding of belief in yourself, in your life and, if you have fallen away, in your relationship with the Divine.

It has been said that faith is not belief without proof, but rather Trust without reservation, and that Trust, when cared for and respected, encourages the self to blossom. Trust is divine medicine.

For some, drawing this Rune asks you to show Trust in a present situation. For others, it calls for embracing the changes you are facing with Trust and wisdom.

If this Rune applies to your relationship with yourself, know that love grows when Trust is present. And in relationships of the heart, remember that *I love you* and *I trust you* are two stones for crossing the same stream.

On the other hand, if Trust is lacking in your life, consider what you can do to restore it, or to create it where it never was. For Trust is the foundation upon which we build our lives and do God's work in the world. However oppressive or painful the moment may seem, this Rune urges you to have faith and to know that, as you heal, you *will* be able to trust again.

Look at it this way: Each time you face the issue of Trust,

you are being asked to grow. When you push through your fears and trust your feelings, you do grow—and Trust grows in you.

Receiving this Rune, you are encouraged to take the first step, to reclaim the lost Trust you once cherished and thrived upon. We are born to live our lives in Trust. Let no one tell you differently.

Know thyself was the counsel of the Oracle at Delphi in ancient Greece. Now, at the close of the twentieth century, to those wise words let us add: *Trust and heal thyself.*

Persevere in your journey, and trust in your healing process, for both are uniquely yours and as individual as fingerprints and snowflakes.

Whenever this Rune comes to you, remember the wise teacher, the one that speaks from the silence within us.

The breath of heaven is everywhere Trust is.

3. Guilt

In receiving this Rune, remember to let the constraints of the time serve you in righting your relationship with yourself. Use this moment to bring quiet to whatever sense of confusion or sadness you may be feeling. There is nothing you can do to change what has already happened. You can only accept it and turn it over to God.

Guilt feeds on conflict. If this Rune relates to a situation for which you feel blame, all you can ask of yourself is to face what has occurred honestly and directly, and then do whatever you can to resolve the conflict and to restore if not harmony at least balance.

The Rune of Guilt fosters healing by reminding us of the need to make amends. For those who seek to heal situations from the past—for what was done or left undone—this Rune counsels you to open your heart and act. Is there a letter to be written, a call to be made, someone you must sit with face to face, a prayer to be said? Now is the time to bring order, clarity and peace to the chaos of the past.

When taking action to make amends is impossible or inappropriate, amends of the heart are always heard. Often the most profound healings occur when God's words are felt, not spoken.

If it seems the conflict will never be resolved, allow yourself the feelings of powerlessness. Experience your feelings fully—and then release them. Learning how to let go of the things we cannot change is a crucial part of the healing now under way in our world.

If you have received this Rune in response to your concern about a mistake you feel you have made, the Oracle is unambiguous: We all make mistakes. No Guilt need be attached to our mistakes, for this is how we learn. Endless self-blame has no place in healing.

The anxiety engendered by Guilt shakes our trust, distorts our judgments and clouds our perceptions. For to live with Guilt is to sabotage the self. Guilt is a dragon that guards the toxic waste of the past.

If, on the other hand, you are feeling no Guilt, you may be wondering why you picked this Rune. Perhaps you picked it so that you might consider the question of the restoration of faith in our troubled time—the rebuilding of faith in ourselves, faith in those we love, in our families, our friends and our communities.

4. Grief

In drawing this Rune, look to the care of your heart. For the heart is where the deepest memories of Grief are held, and where Grief's wounds will finally be healed.

Rare indeed is the life that has not been touched by Grief. Whether the Grief you are feeling is in the present, or an old sorrow you are now strong enough to face, remember: Without the experience of grieving, you may never move beyond that which has caused you so much sadness, so much pain. Be it the death of a child, a spouse, a friend, a parent gone but never truly mourned—*feel* your Grief and embrace it. For it is in the depths of Grief that we come to know and value life.

Ask yourself if this Rune is a messenger, sent to connect you to the Grief of another, someone who is overwhelmed with grieving and sorely in need of a friend simply to listen or share their tears. Grief wears many masks. Remember this whenever it is the heart of another you are being called to care for.

In regret, grieving takes another form: regret for what was done or left undone, for what was said or never said. The Rune of Grief can serve as a gentle reminder to make amends where you have wronged another, to do or say what you know in your heart will heal the past.

Sometimes feelings of regret and loss arise when we fail to take advantage of an opportunity. We tell ourselves: "It was the chance of a lifetime," and we grieve for what we've missed. In looking back, acknowledge that your path lay elsewhere, and make your peace with what was not to be.

If you have been too long alone with Grief, this Rune is saying, reach out for help to family and friends. Or having neither, find a community that can support and comfort you, a fellowship that will welcome you with understanding.

For some, this Rune announces that the time has come to mourn an old sorrow. For others, it heralds the end of a long period of grieving. Either way, know that even the deepest Grief, when fully felt, will lessen and soften over time. There is a calm to be found on the far side of Grief, a peace unknown to those who have yet to grieve.

If nothing else, receiving this Rune calls us to spend a moment in prayer for the relief of pain, the practice of kindness and the restoration of peace in our troubled world:

We ask in the name of all Thy creatures
That our suffering shall cease;
That we shall be fed and healed
Provided with safe haven here on earth,
And then, oh Divine Mystery, a home in Thee.

5. Gratitude

Practice Gratitude each day for the blessings you receive from God. Be grateful for Divine wisdom and guidance, for the courage to face your pain and for the strength of your spirit. Be thankful for the love in your heart, and the willingness to walk the path of healing.

This Rune is an invitation to count your blessings. Whose love has touched your heart? Are you blessed with good health? Are you being nourished? Do you nourish others? What brings you joy? What gives you peace?

Be grateful that you find yourself in the company of people who are supportive of your life. For each member of the spiritual community, program or fellowship of which you are a part, give thanks.

Show Gratitude to those from whom you seek counsel, those who inspire you to deepen your faith in God and strengthen your belief in yourself. From deep within, know Gratitude for having survived the anguish of the past. If, even now, your life is being challenged and tested, and you have made it through another long and lonely night, be grateful for your victory.

And if the moment comes when you feel there is no one to whom you can turn, know that you are never really alone, and give thanks each day to God for guiding you out of the ashes.

If you are just beginning to heal, be thankful that you have indeed begun. If you are already well along in your healing, be grateful for what you have to share with others. Wherever you find yourself on your path, be grateful even for the things you are unable to change, for they will be your teachers.

Wherever you find beauty—in acts of kindness by another, in the ripple of sunlight on water, in the loving look from an animal friend—practice Gratitude.

There is a calmness to a life lived in Gratitude, a quiet joy. Feelings of Gratitude are indeed the bounty of such a life. So let us join in celebration with John Wesley's lovely hymn of Gratitude:

> *For the beauty of the earth,*
> *For the beauty of the skies,*
> *For the love that from our birth*
> *Over and around us lies,*
> *Lord above, to Thee we raise*
> *This our joyful hymn of grateful praise.*

Practice Gratitude each morning when the sun comes up. And every evening when the sun goes down, practice Gratitude.

6. Love

Love is the language in which God speaks. For when we listen with Love, it is the heart that hears. Receiving this Rune is a simple reminder to listen—to your heart, to those you love and to the still small voice that always speaks with Love.

The ways of Love are often hidden and secret. Yet once initiated into Love's ways, they become our ways. And when that happens, Love is everywhere. Receiving this Rune is a call to look upon your world through the understanding and accepting eyes of Love. It is said that our soul needs Love's eyes in order to see.

If you are just beginning to learn about Love—learning to love yourself, or learning to love another—take time to find new ways to share what you are feeling. Love's presence is easily recognized in a word of praise, an act of acceptance or through the understanding forgiveness brings.

So much is said of Love, yet one thing is certain: Either Love is present in our every act and word, our every thought, or it is not. And to the degree that Love is absent or waning, so too our healing is diminished and postponed. For Love heals people—the ones who give it and the ones who receive it.

Whatever is troubling you, challenging you or awaiting

resolution, this Rune invites you to claim what is yours and let Love in. See no faults, no disharmonies, no reasons for despair; instead, see only the evidence of Love's presence.

For Love is our true heritage, declared so in the innocence of our birth, ours before the beginning. We are the inheritors of what God is—pure Love.

Feel the warmth and radiance of Divine Love filling your heart and streaming forth into the world to touch all creatures great and small.

7. Shame

Shame from the past throws a shadow across today's sun. How long have you been a child of Shame, standing alone outside the schoolyard fence, watching the other children as they play?

Drawing this Rune signals a time when the Shame you have lived with for so long can be understood and healed, dissolved into memories and pictures that belong only to the past.

Many of us still carry the feelings of chaos and uncertainty from a home where no one listened and boundaries were seldom or never honored. Wherever you are in your recovery, take a few moments to remember the first time you recognized the source of your pain. It is our feelings of Shame that damage trust and sabotage self-acceptance. For this reason, facing both known and secret fears is an essential part of healing the Shame that has bound you to your past.

For some, receiving this Rune acknowledges that you have arrived at a place in your recovery where you possess the clarity, the strength and the will to heal your feelings. You are being called to finally open the sealed rooms of exhaustion, aloneness and fear in which you have been living for so long.

Take comfort from this: When the time is right, you will

find the courage to tell just one person what happened—just one. This Rune teaches that a new life is possible, and that you are indeed learning how to live that life.

Imagine a day when you are free from all feelings of Shame. A day when you are no longer suffering from the painful experiences of your childhood, or feeling wounded by the betrayal of those to whom you looked for the guidance that never came. Realize that you have survived your pain, and honor yourself for your commitment to the healing journey. For it is one of self-acceptance, self-love and self-care. A noble journey out of the shadows and into the Light.

8. Faith

Receiving the Rune of Faith is an opportunity both to renew the commitment to your spiritual journey and to rededicate your life to a larger purpose.

We speak of the gift of Faith because that is how Faith comes to us, as a gift. There is no way to buy it, borrow it or prepare for it. After all, how can we prepare for a mystery? Faith is among God's most precious gifts; without it, doubt and fear will surely find us. When Faith is absent, life lacks meaning, while in its presence, the bounty of Divine Love is always to be found. The essence of Faith is in all things.

One of the purest forms of Faith is service, doing God's work on earth. Faith in action is the willingness to deal with life in the sure and certain knowledge that you will learn from your experience, overcome adversity and be healed.

The Faith that promotes healing simply asks you to reach out wholeheartedly to receive the gift of God's love, and claim it as your own. St. Paul said that we walk by faith and not by sight. When you walk by Faith, this Rune is saying, it is impossible to doubt God, yourself, your life or tomorrow.

Faith encourages us to believe that we can make a difference—a difference first in ourselves, and then in the world. It was Gandhi who said that we must *be* the change we wish to see in the world.

9. Denial

Drawing the Rune of Denial is a call once again to take control of your life and begin living it as God intended—consciously, compassionately, joyously and with love.

For many, this is a time of separating paths. The Oracle reminds us that we were not born to live in pain, but rather to transform our lives through a greater understanding of ourselves and the world around us.

This Rune encourages you to admit to yourself, to God and to another the true nature of your pain and your shortcomings. If you are still avoiding the truth of your situation, take this opportunity to remember that it requires hard work, time and understanding to come out of Denial, out of hiding.

If Denial no longer plays a part in your life, and still you received this Rune, you are being asked to have compassion for those around you. Find ways to be of service to family, to friends, to the people with whom you work. It may be as simple as listening and then saying the words: "I understand." Often that is all it takes to bring comfort and renewed strength to a weary or a troubled heart.

The Rune of Denial calls you to look within and take stock, to make a fearless personal and moral inventory of your life. It counsels you to open yourself up and let the Light into a part of your life that has been secret, shut away.

For some, drawing this Rune announces that the time has finally come to end the dance of Denial. One thing is certain about Denial, and it is this: When something within us is disowned, that which is disowned wreaks havoc.

Above all else, remember: Your protection lies in the Divine, in God as you understand God. Let no false boundaries separate you from the Will of Heaven.

A world that recognizes the value of every single life is a world coming out of Denial.

10. Boundaries

Respect and protection for your feelings, your health and your well-being are almost always at issue when you receive the Rune of Boundaries. Calling as it does for drawing lines and setting limits, this Rune announces that the time has come to provide yourself with healthy and appropriate Boundaries within which you can heal.

Perhaps the challenge you are now facing requires the courage to say no to something that no longer has a place in your life. Boundaries and walls are very different things. As you decide what to accept and what to reject, you will learn to live feeling protected, and yet free of walls.

Drawing this Rune can be an affirmation: *Setting appropriate limits creates freedom.* Cherish your ability to do this, since good Boundaries are essential to developing healthy feelings about yourself. In the Circle of the Runes, healthy Boundaries always bear witness to the fact that someone has courageously undertaken the journey from Denial to Honesty.

When we were younger, the word "boundary" meant limitation. With the maturity of time, we can recognize that good Boundaries create safe harbors in which to change, to heal and to grow.

Receiving this Rune is a reminder to run a reality check.

Are the Boundaries you have established being recognized and respected? On the other hand, are you being sensitive in respecting the Boundaries of those you love and those with whom you work: your family, your friends, your colleagues and *especially* your children?

Like well-tended gardens, sound Boundaries need attention and care, for without well-maintained Boundaries, there can be no safe passage to a new life.

Let it be said this way: Family values crumble and fall away without the support of healthy Boundaries. In their absence, our ability to teach our children to respect us and each other is weakened. Good Boundaries provide a shade tree, a learning tree, under which our children and our children's children will gather the knowledge that they will then pass on to future generations.

11. Honesty

The sacred hand mirror of truth now lies in front of you. Pick it up in silence and, without fear, look into your present situation. Ask if you are being honest, first with yourself, and then with others. To be honest with one's self is where all healing begins.

If you are only now learning the simplicity that is born of true Honesty, take a moment to remember the very first time you admitted to yourself or to another the depth and truth of your feelings. Be grateful for the relief you felt and the wisdom you gained by laying down the burden you had carried for so long.

For some, drawing this Rune is a sign that the days of hiding from yourself and from others are over. If, however, those days are still upon you, meditate on Shakespeare's poignant words, *This above all: To thine own self be true.*

Honesty opens locked cupboards in the heart. Being honest is one way of relieving the pain. If you find that speaking the truth is still difficult, perhaps the very reason you received this Rune is to remind you to ask God for the courage to try again.

Consider, if you will, Honesty's position on the Circle of the Runes. Between Boundaries and Serenity, the Oracle is saying, lies the frontier of Honesty. Once you reach this place, life is easier, for it takes less effort to be honest than dishonest. When you deal honestly with life, your body and your heart will create Boundaries for you—Boundaries that support you while you take the steps to change—and step by step, Serenity will become an ever greater part of your life.

Receiving this Rune, you are reminded that there is less of everything—less hope, less trust, less faith, less to life itself—without rigorous Honesty. The moment has come, this Rune is saying, to make a searching and fearless moral inventory of your feelings, your ways of thinking and your actions. And to remember that, when Honesty goes, it takes Serenity with it, for the seeds of the courage to heal can only grow in honest soil.

It has been said that among the attributes of the well-nourished self are the ability and the willingness to nourish others. Honesty nourishes the soul even as it fosters healing.

As the years go by and the course of our life changes, it is the ability to be honest with ourselves that provides us with the opportunity to teach the next generation that there is both honor and power in speaking the truth.

12. Serenity

Receiving this Rune is recognition of how far you have come along the path of healing. Give thanks to God for the blessings Serenity brings. In the past, we hardly knew this peaceful place, with its freedom from want and need. It is through a life lived in Serenity that we come to know and understand our closeness to the Divine.

Serenity is a fruit-bearing branch from the tree whose roots bind up all the Runes: Honesty leads to Serenity, and Patience issues from it. Grief, Anger and Fear are resolved in its embrace, while Trust and Faith are nourished by Serenity and Love thrives in its presence.

There is a place inside our being where Serenity dwells. Take time each day to nourish yourself with the comfort to be found there. For it is from this place of tranquillity and peace that all service begins. Become familiar with what Serenity means in your daily life.

Without Serenity, wounds are slow to heal, while in its presence, all things are possible. If Serenity is absent from your world, and you are still riding the merry-go-round of chaos and denial, ask the Divine for the guidance and strength to face your life with courage. And if you feel your Serenity slipping away, know that God will restore it to you through the power of prayer. Pause for a moment and remember above all to stay present and live your life one day, one moment, at a time. The clear and simple message of this Rune is: *Practice Serenity.*

The beauty and power of Serenity are expressed in a prayer adapted from the words of Reinhold Niebuhr, words read and spoken daily by millions of people all over the world:

> *God grant me the serenity to accept the things I cannot change, the courage to change the things I can, and the wisdom to know the difference.*

This prayer is a gift containing all the elements of Divine Love. When you allow Serenity to fill your days and your nights, you have truly begun to heal your life.

13. Patience

Happy is the one whose own heart never lies, who knows what waiting means and still can wait.

In drawing this Rune, you are being asked to show Patience in some part of your life. If you are one who has endless Patience for others and almost none for yourself, this Rune is a reminder: Since the starting place for healing and recovery is always the self, take time each day to give yourself the gift of Patience. Acknowledge and appreciate your own efforts, and be grateful for your progress along the path of growth and healing.

St. Thomas Aquinas reminds us that Patience is part of courage, and that sometimes courage requires us to wait. When you are healing, you must allow each step to take place in its own time. With the practice of Patience come perseverance, trust and wisdom. Judging, comparing, needing to know why—these are never your allies. Patience is your ally.

If you have just received difficult or troubling news, find a quiet place to be with what you've learned. Consider whether the situation you are facing is part of life's endless coming to be and passing away, or part of that which abides. Then turn your troubles over to God. Even in our darkest hours,

Patience speaks to us and comforts us, saying: *This too shall pass*.

For some of us, receiving this Rune serves as a reminder that, as with all things, Patience too has its healthy limits. Whatever the case may be, you are encouraged to learn the difference between Patience and denial. If in your present situation you have been patient too long, then Patience is no longer a virtue.

What stronger evidence can there be that you are truly healing than your willingness to live your life patiently, consciously, one day at a time? As you contemplate this Rune, remember that the Will of Heaven is at work in your life, and that Patience is one of Love's master teachers.

By adding Patience to Serenity, you will reach a place of Acceptance, and you will look with serene eyes upon a world that no longer withholds from you the love you were born to receive. Be mindful that Patience is essential for the recognition of your own process which, in its season, leads to the harvest of the self.

14. Acceptance

This is a Rune of major blessings, blessings received and blessings bestowed. Acceptance forms the foundation for loving yourself. Before you can rebuild your life, you must come to know the peace that accompanies self-acceptance, for out of that peace arises the wisdom and the willingness to greet each day with a quiet heart.

In the circle of God's wisdom, Serenity and Acceptance are linked by Patience. Serenity and Acceptance are twins. Yet, as with all twins, one must be born first, one second; one leading, one following. To be a happy second twin is to understand the true nature of Acceptance.

Therefore, waste not a moment to invoke the Serenity Prayer:

> *God grant me the serenity to accept the things I cannot change, the courage to change the things I can, and the wisdom to know the difference.*

Whatever may be troubling you, this Rune is saying, know that the time has come to accept what you cannot change, especially if it has caused you confusion, sorrow or pain. To do so restores to you the power to change what you can. If you feel the pain is too great, you may need to turn to prayer in order to find your way to Acceptance. And yet sometimes it is unwise to pray away the pain, lest the understanding to be gained on the far side of pain be prayed away, too.

For it is the gradual Acceptance of the feelings and memories of the past that enables us to change. And while you may be unable to alter your present situation, what you *can* do is transform your response to that situation. Herein lies your freedom—a freedom that will, in time, permit you to move on.

Remember that you are a human being, this Rune is saying. Embrace your imperfections and know that you can set a new course for your life, one degree at a time, one day at a time.

Here is a thought so simple that it might seem trivial, and yet it lies at the heart of Acceptance: *Where you are now is just fine, because that's where you are, and you have a perfect right to be there.* Anyone who is reluctant to support you in being where you are, at this moment, is no friend of Acceptance.

There is a special kind of valor in accepting the truth of what is happening in our lives, our families, our schools, our cities and our nation. For until we can teach our children the power of Acceptance, there is neither the possibility for lasting change, nor any hope to alter the course of human events in the years to come.

Receiving this Rune calls for gladly giving up the old and being prepared to live, for a while, empty, while you wait for the new to become illuminated in its proper time.

15. Courage ↑

Courage is faith in action. Drawing this Rune indicates that you are being asked to recognize and honor the Courage and strength of your own spirit. As you do, you will grow in the understanding necessary to continue traveling the road you have chosen, and to face with wisdom whatever challenges life brings.

Anyone who has been sorely tested—suffered through the death of a loved one, been critically ill, recovered from an addiction or broken the silence of spousal abuse—knows well the Courage it takes to heal. The insight from these transforming experiences gives us hope and teaches us that the reward for Courage is wisdom.

If it is the past that troubles you, know that the past is often healed by a courageous heart and mind.

Are you are being asked to make a leap of faith into an uncertain future? If so, consider the Circle of the Runes, where Courage lies between Acceptance and Prayer. Thus, the Oracle is saying: If you react to the present situation with panic or denial, there is no place for Courage to take hold. If the challenge confronting you feels overwhelming, think upon those who have faced great adversity with grace, and pray for their example to inspire you.

Time and again, the true test of Courage is to live rather than to die, to survive the period of crisis and complete your healing. Take comfort also from this: There is intimacy with the Divine arising from the small brave acts that help us through each day.

For some, receiving this Rune may be a reminder to reach out and ask for help. Taking the risk of reaching out is one of those brave acts of daily Courage. For others, the Rune of Courage announces that the cycle of sorrow and pain has finally come to an end. Be at peace with your healing. You have walked the path of true Courage; now it is time to go out in the world and live the life you were born to live.

16. Prayer

You to whom all hearts are open, all secrets known, hear our prayers.

The proper prelude to all things is Prayer, for it is through Prayer that we practice the Presence of God in our lives.

Whatever your concern may be, place it in the hands of the Divine through Prayer. For Prayer nourishes with love the good desires of the heart; it quiets the troubled spirit and summons to our cause the highest good for all concerned. Each time our actions are blessed by Prayer, we invite the Divine to share in our dedication and give us joy.

With nothing in our hands to which we cling, with listening minds and lifted hearts, we pray.

The Rune of Prayer is always a timely reminder: Pray when you feel uncertain, fearful or alone. Pray for the well-being of those you love. Pray for your leaders, your country and for the survival of Mother Earth.

We ask that Prayer be second nature to us now, deeper than a habit, the very heartbriar of our lives.

Receiving this Rune, we pray for healing. For the healing of childhood wounds and the addictions they engendered. We ask for the healing of our bodies, our minds and our hearts. For the righting of injustices, and the mending of damaged lives.

From deep within our hearts, we pray for the permanent cessation of violence and an end to all abuse. We pray for Love and Light to come and seal the door where evil dwells.

Above all, we pray for the precious care of our souls.

With our every Prayer, let us ceaselessly and tirelessly pray for the lives of our children.

Among the sweetest of all are Prayers of gratitude and thanksgiving. From all cultures, all peoples, all directions, we come bringing our Prayers of homage and devotion.

We pray, and our Prayers turn to praise upon our lips.

No matter what is happening in your life, this Rune is saying, take time to offer up your Prayers. And know this, as surely as you know anything: Even when you are not speaking to God in Prayer, God hears. Your every breath is a Prayer.

Practice the Presence of God in all ways, both in your coming in and your going out.

17. Forgiveness

A life in transition draws upon Forgiveness in order to make peace with the past. Receiving this Rune, you are asked to consider: Who is it that calls out to you for Forgiveness? To whom do you call out?

To all of you who find the courage in your heart to forgive those who betrayed you, this Rune brings a blessing.

Forgiving someone who hurt you, and making amends—these are two faces of Forgiveness. There is a third face as well: Consider whether receiving this Rune, at this moment, may be an invitation to extend Forgiveness to yourself.

Drawing the Rune of Forgiveness is an opportunity to consider the situations in your life where you have been thoughtless, unkind or mean-spirited. What can you do to make amends? Do you need to write a letter, sit face to face, or simply speak openly to that person, ask for their Forgiveness and give them your blessing?

It has been said that to cling to resentment is to harbor a thief in your heart. For resentment robs you of your energy, your strength, your peace of mind and, ultimately, your ability to heal. It is not part of our nature to withhold Forgiveness.

And yet, to those of you for whom Forgiveness is impossible, this Rune brings a double blessing: one for the courage it took to close the door on the past; another for your willingness to go on and live your life.

There is one more blessing in this Rune. It is for those who have the courage to brave the fearsome seas of anger and rage and, in time, arrive upon Forgiveness' safe shore.

Take this moment, the Rune of Forgiveness counsels, to begin cleaning out the old. And if you have already begun, be gentle with yourself, it takes time to release the past.

Let it be said this way: *As I cultivate my own nature, all else follows.*

This Rune would be incomplete without an image of Forgiveness as the scales upon which our lives are balanced: *Joy in forgiving, and joy at being forgiven, hang level in the balances of love.*

18. Humor

Drawing the Rune of Humor is always an encouraging sign, for Humor is really three Runes in one: an Invitation, a bit of Advice and a Blessing.

If you find yourself in the middle of a difficult situation which threatens to overwhelm you, take time out to see the Humor in it all. That's the Invitation.

The Advice goes something like this: Pushing yourself too hard? Doing too much for others? Break the pattern. Have a giggle. Lighten up. And always remember: Humor is the mildest detergent of them all.

Since it is said that God's favorite music is laughter, know that each time you laugh, your laughter is your gift to God. That's the Blessing.

If you are just now recovering your sense of Humor, this Rune congratulates you. If, on the other hand, you're convinced that your Humor has gone, the Oracle is saying: *No need to worry, it will return as you heal.* For Humor is healing's handmaiden.

Humor springs from the Rune of Flow. Flow is the softest, most feminine of the older Runes, calling as it does for contacting your intuitive wisdom and attuning to your own rhythms. If you are out of harmony with your healing, this

Rune is saying: Humor will help you to restore the balance.

It is on the road to healing that we recover our sense of Humor and learn to apply the salve of laughter to old wounds. Good Humor is indeed good medicine. The ability to laugh at oneself is always a healthy sign. Laughter delights the soul and brings joy to the heart; it adds flavor to gratitude, lessens the burden of our mistakes, turns enemies into friends, dissolves fear and, in so doing, encourages love.

The ancients equated laughter with wisdom and with heaven's will. It has been well and truly said that the day most wholly lost is the day on which we do not laugh.

Humor and laughter are hallmarks of our humanness.

19. Anger

The challenge for you in drawing the Rune of Anger is to take Anger's powerful energy and treat it as an ally in your healing, a wake-up call for change.

This Rune announces that the moment has come for you to let go of Anger. Know that in doing so you must give up the old and be willing to wait patiently for the new to be revealed to you in its proper time.

Be mindful that there are situations in which Anger can serve as a signal from within, a warning that something in your life is out of balance, unexamined or crying out for attention. In drawing the Rune of Anger, you are being asked to consider this possibility.

Since Anger is often a mask for hurt, fear or feelings of abandonment, look beneath your Anger and ask yourself: Are you feeling angry because you feel no one is listening, because it seems that no one sees you or because you have no one to turn to? Has some aspect of the present situation caused fresh pain in an old wound? Whatever may be the case, welcome Anger as information. Explore it, see where it is coming from and how it prevents you from saying what you truly mean to say.

Receiving this Rune need not be taken as a challenge or a

demand that you face your Anger. In fact, you needn't even be angry to draw the Rune of Anger.

Each Rune offers you an opportunity for meditation. So take time to think about your circumstances. Meditate on your Anger. See if you can find a safe passage that leads from the present situation to a place of harmony and peace.

Anger at injustice can be a liberating and powerful force for change. Healthy Anger, appropriate Anger, can free you to break old patterns of helplessness. Anger is a force that can provide you with the energy to change.

There is a blessing for you in receiving this Rune, a new way of looking at life, a new way of responding to conflict. When you are able to take that new perspective out into the world, surely then you can call Anger your teacher and your friend.

20. Surrender

It is through Surrender that we come to recognize a force greater than ourselves, a limitless Power that is available to us, a Power that heals. Surrender is the highest form of conscious contact with the Divine.

Almost all of the world's great religions and spiritual paths practice some form of Surrender. Drawing this Rune is an invitation to turn your will and your life over to God.

Not so long ago, Surrender meant defeat and brought with it shame and dishonor. On the healing journey, Surrender means relinquishing control, for in so doing we acknowledge our readiness to heal.

Receiving this Rune, you are being asked to let go of your need to control the present situation, or to release any past experience that continues to trouble you.

For some, this Rune encourages your Surrender to the feelings of being alone or abandoned by embracing your fears and moving through them hand in hand with the Divine.

If you are facing a critical illness, a life crisis, or if the moment has finally come to stop fighting yourself, be grateful, and practice Surrender. And if you do nothing else, *Let go and let God.* For many of us, this oft-repeated phrase has already provided safe passage to a new way of life. If you are seeing these words for the first time, let them mark a new beginning for your healing.

The true power of Surrender always changes our lives.

Since this Rune has come to you this day, pray and affirm: *I surrender my will to the Greater Will, the Will of the Divine. I will to will Thy Will.*

21. Wisdom

It has been said that Wisdom is a map upon which to follow the journey of the spirit, a sacred text of understanding from which to learn about the care of the soul.

The ability to accept and grow from life's lessons is the beginning of Wisdom. As Wisdom deepens, it lends inspiration to creativity and understanding to grief. The greatest good, said St. Augustine, is Wisdom.

Each time you receive this Rune, take a quiet moment in the midst of the day's occupations. Consider the issue at hand, try to see it in a fresh way. Is it part of the endless coming to be and passing away, or part of that which abides? To know the difference is to see with the eyes of Wisdom.

Oftentimes, when we ask life for answers, God gives us Wisdom. For when there is no immediate answer, Heaven provides us with another way of seeing the situation, and it is out of that new vision that our choices and our paths become clearer.

It is through Wisdom that a tragedy becomes a teaching. That is Wisdom's way—and love's way. For it is Wisdom that teaches the mind to understand and learn through love.

Drawing this Rune is always a gift, urging us, as it does, to remember these comforting words: *Wisdom is precious. Wisdom is earned. The wise do not need to speak for their wisdom to reveal itself. It is their love and understanding that heal us.*

As we grow in Wisdom, we learn to seek our counsel and our comfort in the Will of Heaven.

22. Hope

Hope is a light that never fails, a flame burning in the darkest night, an elusive feeling that urges you on when, against all reason, you refuse to give up. Hope is among the most abiding of God's gifts.

It has been said that in each life, there comes at least one moment which, if recognized and seized, transforms the course of that life forever. Have there been special moments when Hope came to you? What brought Hope into your life? Was it your desire for a quiet, grounded, more centered existence? Was it your yearning for a better future in a peaceful world? Or was it a broken heart? Whatever the reason, once it returns, Hope restores our optimism that tomorrow can mark a new beginning.

What would bring you Hope this day? Perhaps something as simple as caring words from a loving friend, or taking that first step, or another day of sobriety. Whatever form of inspiration will nourish your spirit, hold it with care in loving hands.

If you are concerned about your health, remember that through the eyes of Hope, even illness can be seen as a gift, an opportunity to acquire the wisdom born of adversity. Embrace this opportunity, and bind it with your faith. With

Hope, we learn to keep on living our lives courageously and diligently.

If this Rune comes to you as you are entering a new relationship, be mindful to let the lessons you have learned from the past serve you in what is to come. And if your life is moving in a new direction, let yourself feel the Hope that accompanies all new beginnings.

Hope is a companion on our journey, one that whispers in our ear: *It is going to be better . . . The darkness is behind you . . . The daylight has come.*

Rather than collapse yourself into thoughts of the future, stay in the present, for considerable hard work is involved in a time of healing and transformation.

Beyond the suffering and oppression that burden our humanity, we lay claim to our inheritance of Hope.

For so many, throughout the world, Hope is all that remains. Even those who have left everything behind to make a difficult and arduous journey in search of freedom, carry with them their Hope of a better life.

We have all known periods of hopelessness and despair. It is only when we begin to realize that we can no longer continue living in the old way, and come to believe in something greater than ourselves, that hopelessness turns into Hope.

Hope is God's Love at work in our lives.

23. Fear

Patience invites healing as a beautiful landscape calms a troubled spirit. In drawing the Rune of Fear, it is well to remember that Fear usually carries with it a self-fulfilling prophecy. Do not be dismayed. Have patience with your healing.

The Divine uses Fear, the Oracle is saying, to give you what you need. Where Fear still grips your life, there you will find your victories.

Is it Fear that keeps you from making a decision in your present situation? Remember that if left unchecked, healthy doubts grow into irrational fears that stop our lives and cause us senseless confusion, doubt and pain.

Does Fear of failure torment you? Fear of success? Have you been living your life fearing that the cries and whispers of the past will never be silent? Take heart, this Rune counsels, and know that these are only voices from the past.

For those of you who were children of abuse, Fear was your heritage; it clouded everything. But that is no longer the case. This Rune is a gentle reminder to acknowledge the power of change.

Notice where Fear lies on the Circle of the Runes: Behind it comes Hope, and ahead, Compassion waits. What more perfect situation in which to heal our fears? At day's end, this Rune comes softly; it whispers in our ear and warns us not to sleep away good lives as hostages to Fear.

24. Compassion

It has been said that when we have Compassion for one another, we shall be of one mind. For in living a compassionate life, we are practicing the Presence of God in a simple and universal way. Drawing this Rune reminds us to take time to show Compassion to those we meet along our way.

Many of Compassion's qualities are found in other Runes. They shine in Forgiveness, Trust and Love, all of which weave together in the Wholeness to which our nature aspires.

If a family member or friend is sick or sorely troubled, drawing this Rune indicates an opportunity for you to show your Compassion through service.

For some, receiving this Rune calls for a profound recognition: admitting to yourself something that you have long denied. At such a challenging time, remember to have Compassion for yourself.

If you are involved in physical healing, notice that in the Circle of the Runes, Compassion lies between Fear and The Divine. As if to say that Fear, passing through the prism of Compassion, is transformed into the energy and radiance of Love.

To the compassionate self, this Rune is a gentle reminder that the journey to wholeness is just that, a journey. Along the way, in your meditations and your prayers, ask to see the world through compassionate eyes.

25. The Divine

Divine Love is present in each of the seasons of the heart. Throughout our lives, that Love nurtures us, comforts us, inspires and teaches us and, at the end, calls us home.

When did you first begin to know the Divine? Was it in the innocence of your childhood? Was it through adversity or loss that you began your search? Or have you always known there was a Power greater than yourself guiding your life?

Through all of the world's religions—from temples and churches, from mesas and mountain tops—the Divine speaks to us. For some, the Divine dwells only within; for others, God is present everywhere. Consider the poet's call to see God in a blade of grass. How much more wonderful to see God in the face of another human being?

Receiving this Rune is a gentle reminder to hold yourself in the Presence of God each day. If the night is long, and you have been sitting alone at the bedside of a troubled or dying loved one, know this: In a still, small voice, God speaks when we are ready to hear. And if you are in the season that calls for reconciling your life, remember that acceptance and forgiveness are two of the greatest teachers of them all.

If you find yourself facing a test for which you feel unwilling or unready, make the Divine your strength. What you are is God's gift to you; what you make of yourself is your gift to God.

Our lives are ordered for us by the Divine so that nothing is too much. Yet if the present challenge seems too great, and you are too weary to travel further, bless this moment and turn your will over to God. As you do so, all else falls away; your burden will be lifted from you, and you will find the courage to go on.

God is physician to all our healing.

However the Divine enters your life—in your love for a child, a partner or for our Mother Earth—God's love is the deepest truth available to us. Once you have made this truth your own, you need never want, never fear again.

And at the end, it is God who calls us home:

I am the Life and the Light and the Way.

The earth is My garden. Each of the souls I plant as seeds germinates and flowers in its season, and in each I am fulfilled. There is no cause for grief when a blossom fades, but only rejoicing for the beauty it held and praise that My will is done and My plan served.

I am one with all creatures and none is ever lost but only restored to Me, having never left Me at all. For what is Eternal cannot be separated from its source.

Meditation on Commitment

There is only one real issue: Why, this day, are you so afraid of making the Commitment? Once made, it doesn't go unheard. And there are consequences for not honoring it. You could literally close your eyes and say: "I'm committed to serving the Source. It's a door I'm walking through right now, and I'm never going back."

Let go of all worry. By not worrying about yourself, Something worries for you. You're just serving. And whatever the vow is, take it fresh every day. Say to the Divine: "This is Your day. I'm going to live it for You."

It only works if you renew it each day.

—Akshara Noor
Diaries

Pastoral Authority 8

Apprehend God in all things
  for God is in all things.
Every single creature is full of God
  and is a book about God.
Every creature is a word of God.

—Meister Eckhart

Some of you come to *The Healing Runes* knowing next to nothing about the oracular, familiar with "runes" only as a crossword puzzle word, if at all. Many of you have strongly defined religious and spiritual traditions of your own. Powerful belief systems sometimes cast shadows that cause the Runes to appear to the faithful as other than what they truly are: a tool for Recovery in the service of the Divine.

My friend Dr. Wallace K. Reid, formerly pastor of the Littlefield Baptist Church, Littleton, Massachusetts, emerged from just such a shadow. An Evangelical Christian, Reid was both unfamiliar with the Runes and suspicious. Nonetheless, he undertook to write a preface to my last book.* In his search for scriptural authority to authenticate, for himself, the use of the Runes as an Oracle, he expressed thoughts and feelings

---

*Ralph H. Blum, *The Book of RuneCards* (New York: St. Martin's Press, 1989).

that may help some of you in resolving your own personal uncertainties and concerns.

The following is an excerpt from Dr. Reid's Preface:

Deep in the collective unconscious of humanity—and perhaps in its very heart—lies the desire to worship a revealing God who will disclose to believers everything they need to know for living a full and productive life.

And to that end, each religion has a place for the oracular. An Oracle can be a Divine saying and/or a vehicle for discerning Divine Wisdom. The *Urim* and *Thummin* of the Old Testament are translated as "Lights and Perfections." They have been described as probably two gemstones placed on the breastplate of the high priest and used in an oracular manner to discern God's will in difficult decisions.

In the New Testament, the Greek word for the oracular is *logia,* meaning short sayings or communications from God, as well as the process or channels through which God reveals Himself. The choosing of a disciple to replace Judas Iscariot was accomplished by oracular means—the drawing of lots.

Considering all the above, I now come to Ralph Blum and the Runes. Are they, the Runes, lights and perfections of the Divine? Or are they of divination as explained in Deuteronomy 18:10–12? I take Scripture seriously, and any knowledge concerning things of the future, I reject. Moreover, I have been very suspicious, as an Evangelical Christian, of any vehicle which claims to have special wisdom from the Divine, wisdom which I cannot ascertain from my prayer life with the Holy Spirit.

My first and second impression of the Runes was one of dismissal. I saw them as a pagan, ancient tool of superstition for insecure people.

And yet, over the twenty-five years that Ralph Blum and I have loved each other as brothers, I have watched his quest and pilgrimage to discern the *Urim, Logia* and Wisdom of the Divine.

So how can I resolve my deep distrust of divination with my deep love for Ralph Blum? This was my particular dilemma when I visited him in January, 1989. I was acutely aware of my discomfort as I walked the beach in Malibu that first evening. Later I studied the Scriptures, then slept restlessly all night at his home over the water and sand. The next morning I arose with confidence, at peace with my answer.

The word came from I Peter 4:11. The text became for me a litmus test for the legitimacy of the Runes. To paraphrase I Peter: *All things oracular must be used to the end that God may be glorified in all things.* Peter counseled Christians to use the oracular with gravity and authority, as a transmission of divine truth rather than for the gratification of personal desires. What words of wisdom! Good counsel for any reader, especially for this skeptical yet loving friend of Ralph Blum.

Listen: I am persuaded that God desires His Will to be made known to creation. To do so is to honor the light. I am convinced that Divine Will *is* discernible, and that the map God reveals to us supports our *stand in the present* and our *walk in the future* . . . My prayer for you who are practitioners of the Runes is that you will use this oracular device with gravity and authority.

I am not a disciple of the Runes. I am, however, a loving disciple of God, His *Urim, Logia* and Wisdom. For me, then, the oracular *is* scriptural. As such, it need not be limited and sealed within the sacred texts of the first century, let alone buried with the Germanic and Viking traditions. The Divine lives and so does The Word.

The Ultimate Art

Followers of Tao use patterns when planning. They observe the ways of nature, perceive the invisible lines of destiny. They imagine a pattern for their entire lives, and in this way, they ensure overall success. . . .

When unpredictable things happen, those who follow Tao are also skilled at improvisation. If circumstances deny them, they change immediately. . . . The spontaneous creation of new patterns is their ultimate art.

—Deng Ming-Dao
365 Tao: Daily Meditations

New Runes for Old Friends

Those of you who are familiar with *The Book of Runes* will have noticed how far this new Oracle has migrated from its roots. There are five distinguishing features to the Healing Runes, three of them minor, two major: We do not use the old Germanic and Norse names as we once did. The Runes now read in the conventional direction (left to right). There are no "Reversed" readings. And most important by far, both the Rune names and the Interpretations are entirely new.

Clearly, what was called for was to *progress* the meanings: Move from a compass for spiritual guidance, to a set of tools for the healing of body, mind, heart and soul. (See page 131.)

Each of my books after *The Book of Runes* has faced a similar challenge: to provide a text that would inform and instruct newcomers, and yet not seem unduly repetitive or tedious to those familiar with the earlier texts. Those of you who work regularly with the Viking Runes will, no doubt, have noted that this book proceeds as if the reader is coming to Runes—perhaps to the oracular as well—for the very first time.

The big question for me, however, concerned my practice with the Oracle. In the end, it boils down to this: When I am starting my day, and I want to touch base with the Divine, hear a runic weather forecast for this day, which Rune Interpretations shall I consult? Those from *The Book of Runes* or those from this work? For quite a while, I did both, randomly, without imposing a pattern or a program.

My conclusion is this: For the ordinary compass checks

in life, like shooting the sun at midday, for the Rule of Right Action for the day or the situation, I turn to *The Book of Runes.*

For challenges or issues bearing upon my healing or the healing of others—the repair of old wounds, the condition of the emotions, the care of the heart, the nourishment of the soul—I turn directly to the new set of Interpretations found in *The Healing Runes.*

Sometimes I consult both, as in the past, I would inquire of two different Oracles to get a broader perspective on an issue. Nowadays, I will consult both the Viking Runes and the Healing Runes on issues that involve the well-being of others, challenges where I have only partial information, or where the situation is critical, and I must act. It is then that I operate on the assumption that some aspects of life can be better understood when insights intersect.

Before writing this chapter on the issue of the relationship between the two sets of interpretations, for example, I decided to consult both oracular systems; to do what one friend calls "The Daily Double." So I found in my storeroom a dusty blue suede bag containing Runes cut from the wooden bones of a ninth-century Norwegian stave church: smoky, dark, wooden Runes I had not touched in many years.

I prayed and gave thanks, then I put my hand in the bag and drew ⋈: by the old reckoning, the Rune of *Partnership;* the Rune of *Trust* by the new. *Partnership* evolving into *Trust.* Both readings with their eyes turned to the Divine. "God always enters into equal partnerships," says the former, and the latter closes: *"The breath of heaven is everywhere Trust is."*

So it appears that the two Oracles can work together toward a common goal, that God may be glorified in all things.

The Healing Runes

The Viking Runes		*The Healing Runes*
The Self	ᛗ	Innocence
Partnership	ᚷ	Trust
Signals	ᚠ	Guilt
Separation	ᚱ	Grief
Strength	ᚢ	Gratitude
Initiation	ᛈ	Love
Constraint	ᚾ	Shame
Fertility	ᛝ	Faith
Defense	ᛇ	Denial
Protection	ᛉ	Boundaries
Possessions	ᚠ	Honesty
Joy	ᚹ	Serenity
Harvest	ᛃ	Patience
Opening	ᚲ	Acceptance
Warrior	ᛏ	Courage
Growth	ᛒ	Prayer
Movement	ᛗ	Forgiveness
Flow	ᛚ	Humor
Disruption	ᚺ	Anger
Journey	ᚱ	Surrender
Gateway	ᚦ	Wisdom
Breakthrough	ᛞ	Hope
Standstill	ᛁ	Fear
Wholeness	ᛊ	Compassion
The Unknowable	☐	The Divine

African Canticle

All you big things, bless the Lord.
Mount Kilimanjaro and Lake Victoria,
The Rift Valley and the Serengeti Plain,
Fat baobabs and shady mango trees,
All eucalyptus and tamarind trees
Bless the Lord.
Praise and extol Him for ever and ever.

All you tiny things, bless the Lord.
Busy black ants and hopping fleas,
Wriggling tadpoles and mosquito larvae,
Flying locusts and water drops,
Pollen dust and tsetse flies,
Millet seeds and dried dagga
Bless the Lord.
Praise and extol Him for ever and ever.

—Anonymous

Envoi: Thoughts for the Soul

Sum up at night what thou hast done by day,
And in the morning what thou hast to do.
Dress and undress thy soul: mark the decay
And growth of it: if with thy watch, that too
Be down, then wind up both: since we shall be
Most surely judged, make thy accounts agree.

—George Spencer, d. 1534

It's dawn. The work on this manuscript is almost over. Susan is away on Second Mesa among her Hopi family. Malibu is recovering from the floods, and nothing is burning or shaking or sliding. Today is the vernal equinox.

A mated pair of pelicans flies North, low over the water, almost brushing the curl of the rising wave with their wing feathers. As I watch them, I am filled with gratitude for the people that make my life such a rich one.

You may have noticed that there is a soul revival in progress just one tent down from where the Angels are trampolining and pirouetting back into our consciousness in such a pleasing way. Perhaps the restoration of the sacred and healing are one and the same. And it all begins and ends in praise and blessing.

Dress and undress thy soul. . . . If there is any situation that brings home to me the meaning of the phrase "weep for joy," it's when I sit in council with my own soul. And so, at sunrise, on the first day of spring, I want to thank my soul and bless it for a fourfold blessing: For affording me a new vision of God. For providing me with a more generous view of myself. For encouraging in me a sense of my own humanity. And through Susan, for bringing to my attention the opportunity of placing this descendant of ancient Oracles once again in play in service to the Divine.

There is one final blessing of which I am very fond. I leave you with it now. The words are St. Patrick's:

May the strength of God pilot us.
May the power of God preserve us.
May the wisdom of God instruct us.
May the hand of God protect us.
May the way of God direct us.
May the shield of God defend us.

It was the poet William Butler Yeats who said, "In dreams begins responsibility." Perhaps what the Runes do best is train us to pay attention to our dreams and to our responsibilities. At least, that seems to me to be a big part of it.

Gud blessi thig. God bless you all.

Ralph H. Blum

A Wanderer's Prayer

Wanting nothing, how shall I be dismayed?
Grieving for no thing lost or unattained,
Why would I choke on the sharp bones of regret?
I am a guest in this house, thoughtful of my manners,
Mindful of my privileges and so filled with gratitude
That when I pray my prayers turn to praise
   upon my lips.
Were I to die just as I am, surrounded so with beauty,
My soul, returning to its Source, opened wide
And revealing the map of my journey,
Would show forth, undiminished, beauty only,
   only beauty.
And so, Beloved, I have written this poem for You.

                        —RHB

Acknowledgments
—Susan Loughan

I would especially like to thank the following people without whose love, continuous support and understanding *The Healing Runes* might never have been written: My dear friend and soul sister, Andra Akers; my lifelong friends, Marian Simon, Julia Adams and Deena Paulsen; and our lawyer and friend, Jonathan Kirsch. Every time I felt I couldn't go on, they remained optimistic, and encouraging. I shall always be grateful.

My heartfelt thanks to two of the finest public servants I've ever had the pleasure to meet. To Detective Doug Raymond, L.A.P.D., T.M. Unit, for his perceptive guidance, support and friendship during a most difficult time in my life. And to Los Angeles Deputy City Attorney John Wilson (ret.), for his vision and tireless wisdom.

I would particularly like to acknowledge Katie Kemble, Denise McMillan, Ron Botier and my Sonoma County "family" for their love and friendship through the years: Leona Shipley, Lynne Brilhante, Carolyn Baker, Ph.D., Ariana Zimmerman, Caterina Martinico, Daniel Martinico, Joelle Mayton, Sarah Helleskov, David Helleskov, Peggy and Errol Twyford, Doug and Lisa Rice, Sue Nieuwenhuije, Karen Lari, Sue Cambron, Denis Coleman, Jr., Louise Koester, Marjorie Nittinger Parks, Ronda Lumley O'Leary, Nathaniel Sewell, Ryan Salaz, Jaynellen Kovacevich, Raziel Madden, Keersha Winds, Betsy Anderson, Dale Moore, Suzanne Meyers, Patti Bailey, M.D., Mark Lightner, Gary Adams, Suzanne Sullivan, Ron Festine, Stephen Smith, M.A., Ishvanni LeClair, Hugo Armstrong, Lisette Guy, Todd Victor, and the magician himself, Jason Guy.

I have always believed that friends are our chosen family, and to that end a special thanks goes to a small circle of friends in Los Angeles: Anita Byrd, Hector Herrera, Sharon Gless, Susan Simmons, Nancy Lee Andrews, Patti Callicott, Judalon Smyth, Dominick

137

Dunne, Syndi Winter, Richard Margolin, Rafael Kalina, Laura Longoria, Eddie Barnes, Alan Howard, Gaylan Larmore, M.A., Pat Simmons, John Voight, Kelly Cutrone, Jeff Kober, Michael Grais, Laurie Gelman, John Robinson, Ferdinand Califano, Doris Van Cleave, Elva Reagan, Mary Lou Gregg, Darrilyn Butler, Lisa Gordon, Judy Radovsky, Brenda Norman, Lizanne Kutterer, Fredrick Washburn, Camilla Washburn, Riley O'Farrell, Jeffrey Sturdevant, Pat Quinn, Carol Vogel, Nancy Tuthill, Diane Salinger, Jay Levin, Laurence Bennett, Hanay Geigiomah, Chris "Jello" Eustace and Brooks Barton.

A special thanks to a group of women whose friendship changed my life: AnnBeth Kalina, Kathleen Letterie, Elizabeth R. Burr, Barbara Walter, Jill Hanna, Pene Gillen, Amanda diGuilio, Catherine and India Oxenberg, Tara Fields Sullivan, Ph.D., Harley Jane Kozak, Susan Waterman, Becky Hulem and Linda Cowan Mose.

To the gifted therapists and healers from whom I sought counsel, my humble gratitude: Kathleen Robinson, Jonna Lannert, Ph.D., Ron Alexander, Ph.D., Jan Victoria Eisner, P. J. Tyler, Angeles Arrien, Richard Weissman, James Greene III, M.A., Bill Clarke, M.A., Marta Ross, M.A., Lisa Sloan Levin, Cat Politte, Iris Jamgochin, Jim Fickey, M.A., Gary Grimm, M.A., Robert Lorenz, Ph.D. and Colleen McClure, M.A.

To John Renfree, M.D., a lifetime of respect and gratitude for saving my life. A special thanks to Wally Lipp, D.D.S., of Los Angeles, who showed great patience and skill in helping me to learn that pockets of abuse can be found where you least expect them.

Every healer at some point during his or her journey questions the work. It is with a great deal of love and respect that I acknowledge the following people whose personal work on themselves has and always will remain a great source of inspiration to both me and my work: Sheri Herman, Yvette Cantu, Dara Marks, Julie and Petter Barve, Van Ramsey, Alan Howard, Dale Moore, Michael Woods and Pirie Jones Woods, Terry Rogers, Ken Berg, Jim Echerd, Judy Margolis, Jasmine Belenger and Berta Marie Hines, M.D.

Eight years ago I began a great personal journey when I was guided to Second Mesa, one of the great Hopi villages in Northern Arizona. There I found the deepest sense of family I had ever known. It was there that I met the legendary Margaret Coochwytewa. Her love, friendship and guidance forever changed my life. A big piece of my heart lives in Sungopovi Village. To the medicine people, Eva Lomawaima, Jeremy King, Julian Fred and to all the Joseph Family, the Coochwytewa Family, the Dewakuku, the Lomawaima and Tootsie Families. To you all, my humble gratitude for all you have given me and for all I have learned. Finally, my deepest love and friendship to my Hopi sisters Angel Joseph and Tami Tootsie.

I want to acknowledge a most gifted healer and friend, Jeanne Elizabeth Blum, Ralph's dear wife, and the author of *Woman Heal Thyself*, a true companion piece for our work. Without your love, support and friendship, and hundreds of hours at the computer, this project would have been far less strong. I offer you my deep respect and heartfelt gratitude.

Finally, to my dear friend Ralph H. Blum, I thank you especially for your friendship and the strength of your guidance. This has been a truly great learning experience.

Acknowledgments
—Ralph H. Blum

To my father, Ralph H. Blum, a crack shot. To my courageous friend
Liz Rich. And to Bill Mason for his hardnosed editing, wise counsel
and friendship.

My affectionate gratitude goes to many people, and especially to
these: Allan W. Anderson, Lawrence and Kirsten Bloom, Jeffrey
Bronfman, Ted Ravinet, Michael Craft, Helen Divov, Tom Dunne,
Nancy Fox, Amelie Littell, Richard Perl, Minette Rice Edwards, Sally
Richardson, Hayden and Stephan Schwartz, Robert Welsch, Pete
Wolverton and Jeremy Katz (border collies to Blum's restless sheep),
Jaye Zimet and Charles Woods, and to my wise brother, Jack Zim-
merman.

I want to offer special thanks to my particular teachers of soul
business: To Tom Moore for his lovely maintenance manuals, my
favorite among them *Care of the Soul.* To Larry Dossey for his pio-
neering work, *Recovering the Soul: A Scientific & Spiritual Search,* and
for his timely first-aid manual for the soul, *Healing Words: The Power
of Prayer and the Practice of Medicine.* To Matthew Fox for enabling
Meister Eckhart to speak to us and for reminding us that our sense of
the sacred is nurtured in praise. To Deepak Chopra and Robert Bly
for reminding us that the memory of wholeness is, ultimately, the
great healing. To Fred Alan Wolfe for marking the route from quan-
tum to soul. And to Marianne Williamson for continuing to bring all
of us to our feet, excited and applauding.

The oldest unbroken cords of gratitude and affection bind me to
Bronwyn Jones. Even when you are not working full-time on a project, your wisdom and loving good sense continue, uninterrupted by
distance and opinions, to provide the field against which I can better
discern the totality of the work.

140

I am grateful for this collaboration with Susan Loughan. Not only because we have prevailed and brought this new face of the Oracle into the light, but also for what you have taught me about dignity in suffering, good cheer in the face of seemingly nonstop adversity. Yes, and for deepening my understanding of and respect for the courage of those for whom we write.

And how shall I best express my gratitude to my wife, Jeanne Elizabeth Blum? The sight of your first book lying on the table beside my own, and rapidly gaining the light of day, touches me more deeply than any object ever has. I know the suffering that brought you to learn to heal yourself, and to identify and describe a healing system for women that affords them greater sovereignty over their own bodies. Your grace, courage and wisdom are heaven's blessing on my life.

Yes, and particularly to my godchildren, Sebastian Rice Edwards, Sasha Childs, John Michael Spangler and Ildrid Seed.

And then there is my gratitude to the Oracle itself. I have known, almost from the start, that after learning to listen to the Runes, in time, the moment will arrive when we can lay the Runes aside, for we will hear the Voice of the Divine in ourselves. For we will have become the Oracle.

Finally, this book is also for the men in my life.

These are the names of men I especially respect and love; many have been my teachers. Each in his way is a good companion and, long haul or short, I have traveled memorable distances with them all. If you belong in the company, and I slipped up, let me hear from you. If, on the other hand, you are surprised at finding your name in these pages because there remains unfinished business between us, know that a healing is taking place among us all right now, and that I want to make amends.

These then are the names of the men in my life, many still with us, some long gone. I wrote them down as they came to me. I honor them all.

Wesley Hance, Robert Huff, Martin Rayner, Dean Loomos, Alan B. Slifka, Robert Ott, Brother John Maarten Turkstra, Dawson Church, Bill Gladstone, Lessert Moore, Ernest Fetzer, Loren White, Alan W.

Anderson, Mark Gerzon, Gordon Davidson, Peter Lawrence, Ken Heyman, Stephan Ely, James Barclay Harding, Aaron Kipnis, Gene Winick, Jim Channon, Wilton Dillon, Star Lawrence, Adam Kennedy, Frank Duffy, Jim Blechman, Andrew Beath, Alec Vagliano, Howard Wood, Richard Storrs Childs, Jr., David Salmon, Anthony Montague Brown, Llewellyn Williams, Jerry Jampolsky, Gordon Smith, Mike Greenwald, Ken Wapnick, Brian Muldoon, Jerry Parr, Jim Hickman, Jonathan Kirsch, Stephen Xavier, Barry Nugent Head, Bill King, Wilfred Freeman, Brother Anselm, Raimond Frese, John Winston Childs, Pattison Esmiol, Anthony Tancred, Ronnie Pinsler, Ned Davis, Stephen Becker, John Steiner, Father Fechin O'Dougherty, Hamish Hamilton, Jan Werner-Carlson, James Emory Childs, John Wadsworth, Graham Sadd, Terry Hunt, Alan Brooke, Russell Childs, William Shawn, Steven L. Stein, Mark Ivener, Robert Watts, Dick Childs, Francis Huxley, Thomas Saunders, Nigel Pennick, Kijo Morimoto, Jack Faivis, Daniel Maziaraz, Leo Sanchez, Mark Sandrich, John Fairchild, Amal Naj, Kevin Redpath, Tracy Kramer, Giles Mead, Lewey O. Gilstrap, Akani Fletcher, Oscar Dystel, Brugh Joy, Rolf Kammerer, Chuck Mee, Nick Eddison, Ken McCormack, Steve Moses, Robert Howe, Leo Lehman, David Johnston, Wallace K. Reid, Jim Danish, Barton Jay, James Gollen, Jay Levin, Michael Maccoby, Martin Rice Edwards, Robert Henderson, James Adriance, Carl "Starch" Audia, Frank Eventoff, Ray Mardyks, Malik Cotter, Dudley Fitts, Tim Piering, Brian Froud, Robert Gambino, Mark Jaffe, Steve Staples, Robert Lee O'Hare, Paul Hampton, Sydney Lanier, Darrold Murray, Tyrone Power, Jackie Golinor, Rick Paine, Alfred P. Lowman, Tony Day, Chuck Blitz, Peter Freedberger, Christian Reichardt, Ned Leavitt, Leland Stanford Early, David Katzen, Bob Jacobs, Michael Phillips, Jerry Baumring, W. E. R. LaFarge, Steve Bogoff, Josh Marwell, Alan Hunt-Badiner, Harry Haines, Roger Moss, James Coburn, Andre Rosfelder, Phil Schwartz, John Mack, J. Peter Elder, Tomas Collins, Walter Beebe, Christopher Mallaby, Doane Perry, Steve Allen, Robert Gould, Dan Selene, Harry Joe "Cocoa" Brown, Richard Gray Eder, Zion Myers, Les Kassoy, Rob Cowley, Stuart Philip Ross, Roger Rosfelder, John Clausen, Tom McCormack, Berne Clark, Richard Wilbur, Rand deMattei, Julian Plowden, Willard Colston, Michael Murphy, James Seed, Andre Gre-

gory, John Michell, Joe Fergus, Warren Smith, Gary Mittman, Hans
Henderson, Joel Edelman, Anthony Loehnis, Robert Cabot, Peter
Thompkins, Chris Bird, William Pennell Rock, Judson Huss, Fred
Allen Wolfe, Kurt Villadsen, Robert Weil, Robert Gong, Steve
Roberts, Danny Mack, John Keel, Jerry Jampolsky, Knox Burger,
Count Igor Caruso, Adam "Pru" Lewis, Ted Bloecher, David Pomer-
anz, Ed Snedeker, Bob Chartoff, John Pierson, David Anthony Ellis,
Jamie George, Erasmus Barlow, Justin Vagliano, Bryce Bond, David
Womeldorf, Marshall Spangler, Fred Freed, Phillip Rush, Ron Cla-
man, John Romaine, Henry Scammell, Basil Langdon, Bill Bowers,
Kevin Tierney, Harold Nebenzahl, Tracy Kramer, Axel Jensen, Tony
Huston, Robin Gage, Bill Whitsun, Poppy, Timothy Seeger Whelan,
Walter "Buck" Starck, Joel Solomon, Tom Beardon, Takeshi
Kinoshita, Alfred W. Schwalberg, Emerald Starr, Andre Vagliano,
Brando Crespi, Sam Dakin, Yuri Borshchevsky, John Appleton,
Harley Swiftdeer, Josh Reynolds, Max Youngstein, John F. Hunt,
David Crane, Jerry Terranova, James K. Cummings, Don Joseph
Clemente, Valentine Gould, Serge Beddingon Behrens, Michael Bam-
ford, Ethan Emery, David Spangler, David Kern, Tim Joukowsky,
John White, Dick Tuck, Ben LaFarge, Peregrine Eliot, Bill Hartley,
Jared Kieling, Bill Barnes, Doug Robbins, Howard Rower, Alec Cast,
Bob Poulson, Josh Mailman, Tad Mann, Ralph Abraham, Tim Banse,
Charlie Kenneth Feldman, Ken Kobayashi, Levent, Hirth Martinez,
Jay Silverberg, Warren Smith, Phil Slater, Danny Selznick, Harold
Bloomfield, Kahlil Gibran, Jeremy Bradford, Peter Sourian, Peter
Ackroyd, Stephan Ahrenberg, Andy Bowers, Father Austin Ford,
William Brasch Watson, Henry Dakin, Charles Adams Platt, Ron
Goldsand, Jim Wanless, Don Campbell, Jerry Goren, Bill Hushion,
Mickey Lemle, Sam Green, Jonathan Cohen, Frank Sontag, David
Hirschfeld, Norman Ackerberg, Brooks Barton, Chester Shure, Simon
Michael Bessie, Tony Bowers, Paul Brenner, Arthur Loeb, Jr., Ray
Bradbury, John H. Finlay, Jr., Neil Coshever, Bobby Moses, Frank
Beach, William J. J. Gordon, Ronnie Laing, Lloyd Jassin, Jeffrey
Bergen, Robin Maynard, Lou Carlino, Ivan Nabokov, Lee Spiegel,
Michael Goldberg, John Alexander, Akasha Levi, William Alfred,
Johnny Avedon, Robert Lorenz, Monte Farber, Robert Muller, David
Friedman, Mickey Laemle, Patrick John Shephard, Michael Arlen,

Don Shoemaker, Gray Walter, Cesere Lombroso, Mark deWolfe Howe, John Findlay, Les Pockell, Robert Hyde, M.D., Jesus Sanchez, Richard Gere, Leo Lerman, Serge Boutourline, Jr., Donald "Sandy" Sandburg, Hart Leavitt, Ian Jackson, David Carradine, William C. Hammond III, Michael Paul, Vladimir Nabokov, P.R.W. Boeth, Eric Wentworth, Kurt Villadsen, Michael Vidor, Cary Tagawa, Bill Thetford, Ned Leavitt, Ken Wapnick, Les Sinclair, Josh Reynolds, Peter Stone, Tim McGuire, Tim Reynolds, Harley Swiftdeer, Bill Whitsun, Roger Richman, Alan Reddin, Neil Coshever, Max Youngstein, Steve Polk, Paul Willen, John Pelzel, Hallam Movius, Greg Pardes, Jerry Dickler, Eric Orr, Ian Masters, Roger Bingham, Kevin Thomas, Bill Roderick, Sergei Sergeiich Boutourline, Terry O'Shea, Vladimir Pozner, Rexford Powell, Jack Ging, Harry Martin, Warner LeRoy, Vladimir Lebedev, Tim Leary, Barry Campbell Good, John Gibbon, John Fairchild, Ned Davis, Bartley Crum, Robert Ducas, Linc Cornell, Newton Arvin, David Dworsky, Daniel Bell, Marcus Broyles, Larry de Bivort, Stephen Bishop, Stan Madson, Phil Thompson, Sam Rice Edwards, Pete McDonald (of Islesboro, Maine), Jaime Babson, Richard Babson, James Johnson Sweeny, John Burt, Vint Lawrence, Eugene Campeau, Arthur Egendorf, Peter Gruhl, Allan Hunt-Badiner, Donald McDaniels, John Hunting, "Terry" Lawrence, Mortie Guterman, Harry Ufland, John Ufland, Christopher Ufland, Pierre Cossette, Jack Gordean, Ned Marin, Holton Rower, John Cossette, Weston Millikin, Randy Slifka, "Sas" Peters, Kimo Peters, Clyde Kluckholn, Bernard Bunn, Richard Rockefeller, Vladimir Kozintsev, Jay Sandrich, Bobby Myers, Adam Seed, Jonas Seed, Peter M. Ralston, . . .

Selected Bibliography

ALCOHOLISM AND SUBSTANCE ABUSE

Alcoholics Anonymous. The Big Book. New York: Alcoholics Anonymous World Services, 1976.

Pass It On: The Story of Bill Wilson and How the AA Message Reached the World. New York: Alcoholics Anonymous World Services, 1984.

Twelve Steps and Twelve Traditions. New York: Alcoholics Anonymous World Services, 1976.

ADULT CHILDREN OF ALCOHOLICS AND
DYSFUNCTIONAL FAMILIES

Black, Claudia. *It Will Never Happen to Me! Children of Alcoholics.* Denver: Mac Publishing, 1981.

Bradshaw, John. *The Family.* Pompano Beach, FL: Health Communications, 1988.

———. *Healing the Shame That Binds You.* Pompano Beach, FL: Health Communications, 1989.

Chopich, Erika, and Margaret Paul. *Healing Your Aloneness.* San Francisco: HarperCollins, 1990.

Earll, Bob. *I Got Tired of Pretending.* Tucson, AZ: Stem Publications, 1988.

Middleton-Moz, Jane, and Lorie Dwinell. *After the Tear: Reclaiming the Personal Losses of Childhood.* Deerfield Beach, FL: Health Communications, 1986.

Miller, Alice. *The Drama of the Gifted Child.* New York: Basic Books, 1981.

Woititz, Janet Geringer. *Adult Children of Alcoholics.* Deerfield Beach,
   FL: Health Communications, 1983.

THE CHILD WITHIN

Bradshaw, John. *The Homecoming.* New York: Bantam Books, 1990.
Whitfield, Charles, M.D. *Healing the Child Within.* Deerfield Beach,
   FL: Health Communications, 1989.

CHILDHOOD/ADULT TRAUMA AND SEXUAL ABUSE

Davis, Laura, and Ellen Bass. *The Courage to Heal: A Guide for Women
   Survivors of Child Sexual Abuse.* New York: Harper Perennial,
   1988.
Gil, Eliana. *Treatment of Adult Survivors of Childhood Abuse.* Walnut
   Creek, CA: Launch Press, 1988.
Herman, Judith. *Trauma and Recovery.* New York: Basic Books,
   1992.
Miller, Alice. *Thou Shalt Not Be Aware: Society's Betrayal of the Child.*
   New York: Farrar Straus, 1984.
———. *Training in Creativity and Destructiveness.* New York: Dou-
   bleday, 1988.

CODEPENDENCY

Beattie, Melody. *Codependent No More.* San Francisco: Harper/Hazle-
   den, 1987.
———. *Beyond Codependency, and Getting Better All the Time.* New
   York: Harper/Hazleden, 1989.
Norwood, Robin. *Women Who Love Too Much.* New York: Pocket
   Books, 1985.
Paul, Jordan, and Margaret Paul. *Do I Have to Give Up Me to Be Loved
   by You?* Minneapolis, MN: Hazleden, 1983.

DEATH AND GRIEVING

Beattie, Melody. *The Lessons of Love.* New York: HarperCollins,
   1994.
Eadie, Betty Jean, with Curtis Taylor. *Embraced by the Light.* Placerville, CA: Gold Leaf Books, 1994.

Kübler-Ross, Elisabeth, M.D. *On Death and Dying*. New York: Macmillan Publishing Company, 1970.

———. *AIDS: The Ultimate Challenge*. New York: Macmillan Publishing Company, 1987.

Levine, Stephan. *Who Dies?* New York: Doubleday and Co., 1989.

———. *Healing into Life and Death*. New York: Doubleday and Co., 1989.

EARTH HEALING

George, James. *Asking for the Earth*. Rockport, ME: Element Books, 1995.

Lovelock, James. *Ages of Gaia: A Biography of Our Loving Earth*. New York: W. W. Norton, 1994.

Roszak, Theodore. *The Voice of the Earth*. New York: Simon & Schuster, 1993.

Sheldrake, Rupert. *The New Science of Life*. Rochester, VT: Park Street Press, 1995.

———. *The Rebirth of Nature*. London: Rider, 1990.

Todd, Nancy Jack, and John Todd. *From Eco-Cities to Living Machines: Principles of Ecological Design*. Berkeley, CA: North Atlantic Books, 1994.

FOOD ISSUES

Chernin, Kim. *The Obsession: Reflections on the Tyranny of Slenderness*. New York: Harper & Row, 1981.

Roth, Geneen. *Feeding the Hungry Heart: The Experience of Compulsive Eating*. New York: New American Library, 1982.

Woodman, Marion. *The Owl Was a Baker's Daughter: Obesity, Anorexia Nervosa and the Repressed Feminine*. Toronto: Inner City Books, 1980.

GENDER ISSUES

Gray, John. *Men Are from Mars, Women Are from Venus*. New York: HarperCollins, 1992.

Kipnis, Aaron, and Elizabeth Herron. *Gender War, Gender Peace: The*

Quest for Love and Justice Between Women and Men. New York: William Morrow & Co., 1994.

Perry, Danaan. *Warriors of the Heart*. Cooperstown, NY: Sunstone Publications, 1991.

Tannen, Deborah. *You Just Don't Understand*. New York: William Morrow & Co., 1990.

Welwood, John. *Journey of the Heart: Intimate Relationships and the Path of Love*. New York: Harper Perennial, 1991.

ILLNESS AND HEALING

Duff, Cat. *The Alchemy of Illness*. San Francisco: HarperCollins, 1993.

Hay, Louise. *You Can Heal Your Life*. Carson, CA: Hay House, Inc., 1984.

James, John, and Frank Cherry. *The Grief Recovery Handbook*. New York: Harper & Row, 1988.

Joy, W. Brugh, M.D. *Joy's Way*. Los Angeles: Jeremy Tarcher, Inc., 1979.

———. *Avalanche*. New York: Ballantine Books, 1990.

Moyers, Bill. *Healing and the Mind*. New York: Doubleday, 1993.

Norwood, Robin. *Why Me, Why This, Why Now: A Guide to Answering Life's Toughest Questions*. New York: Carol Southern Books, 1994.

Peck, M. Scott, M.D. *The Road Less Traveled*. New York: Simon & Schuster, 1978.

Siegel, Bernie S., M.D. *Love, Medicine and Miracles*. New York: Harper Perennial, 1986.

MEN'S HEALING

Abbott, Franklin. *New Men, New Minds*. Freedom, CA: The Crossing Press, 1987.

Bly, Robert. *Iron John*. New York: Random House, 1992.

Harding, Christopher, ed. *Wingspan: Inside the Men's Movement*. New York: St. Martin's Press, 1992.

Johnson, Robert. *He*. New York: HarperCollins, 1989.

Kauth, Bill. *A Circle of Men*. New York: St. Martin's Press, 1992.

Keen, Sam. *Fire in the Belly*. New York: Bantam Books, 1991.

Lee, John. *The Flying Boy: Healing the Wounded Man*. Deerfield Beach, FL: Health Communications, 1989.

Meade, Michael. *Men and Water of Life*. San Francisco: Harper-Collins, 1993.

Monick, Eugene. *Phallos: Sacred Image of the Masculine*. Toronto: Inner City Books, 1987.

Moore, Robert. *King, Warrior, Magician, Lover*. San Francisco: HarperCollins, 1991.

PARENTING

Bethner, Betty Lou, and Amy Len. *Raising Kids Who Can: Using Family Meetings to Nurture Responsible, Cooperative, Caring and Happy Children*. New York: HarperCollins, 1992.

Rich, Adrienne Cecile. *Of Woman Born: Motherhood as Experience and Institution*. New York: Bantam Books, 1977.

SERVING THE SOUL

Bly, Robert. *Loving a Woman in Two Worlds*. New York: Harper-Collins, 1985.

———, James Hillman and Michael Meade, eds. *The Rag and Bone Shop of the Heart*. New York: Harper Perennial, 1992.

Chopra, Deepak. *Ageless Body, Timeless Mind*. New York: Harmony Books, 1993.

———. *The Seven Spiritual Laws of Success*. San Rafael, CA: Amber-Allen Publishing/New World Library, 1994.

Dalby, Gordon. *Healing the Masculine Soul: An Affirming Message for Men and the Women Who Love Them*. Waco, TX: Word Books, 1988.

Deng, Ming-Dao. *365 Tao: Daily Meditations*. San Francisco: Harper SanFrancisco, 1992.

Dossey, Larry, M.D. *Recovering the Soul: A Scientific & Spiritual Search*. New York: Bantam New Age, 1989.

———. *Healing Words: The Power of Prayer and the Practice of Medicine*. San Francisco: Harper SanFrancisco, 1993.

Fox, Mathew. *A Spirituality Named Compassion*. San Francisco: Harper SanFrancisco, 1979.

Harrison, Jane. *Themis*. Cleveland & New York: Meridian Books, 1927.

Kipnis, Aaron. *Knights Without Armor*. Los Angeles: Jeremy P. Tarcher, 1991.

Lowinsky, Naomi R. *Stories from the Motherline: Reclaiming the Mother-Daughter Bond, Finding Our Feminine Souls*. Los Angeles: Jeremy P. Tarcher, 1992.

Moore, Thomas. *Care of the Soul*. New York: HarperCollins, 1992.

———. *Soul Mates*. New York: HarperCollins, 1994.

Rilke, Rainer Maria. *The Best of Rilke*, trans. Walter Arndt. Hanover, NH & London: University Press of New England, 1989.

Teish, Luisah. *Jambalaya: The Natural Woman's Book*. San Francisco: Harper & Row, 1985.

Vanzant, Iyanla. *Acts of Faith: Daily Meditations for People of Color*. New York: A Fireside Book/Simon & Schuster, 1993.

Daily Word. Unity Village, MO: Unity. (Monthly publication.)

Forward Day by Day. Cincinnati, OH: Forward Movement Publications. (Monthly publication.)

WOMEN'S HEALING

Blum, Jeanne Elizabeth. *Woman Heal Thyself: An Ancient Healing System for Contemporary Women*. Boston: Charles E. Tuttle Co., 1995.

Eisler, Riane. *The Chalice and the Blade*. San Francisco: Harper & Row, 1987.

Estes, Clarissa Pinkola. *Women Who Run with the Wolves*. New York: Ballantine Books, 1992.

Freedman, Rita. *Beauty Bound*. Lexington, KY: D.C. Heath and Co., 1986.

Leonard, Linda Schierse. *The Wounded Woman*. Boulder, CO: Shambhala, 1987.

Mankowitz, Ann. *Change of Life: Dreams and Menopause*. Toronto: Inner City Books, 1984.

Scaraf, Maggie. *Intimate Partners*. New York: Ballantine Books, 1987.

Sheehy, Gail. *The Silent Passage*. New York: Pocket Books, 1993.

Tavris, Carol. *The Mismeasure of Woman*. New York: Simon & Schuster, 1992.

Williamson, Marianne. *A Return to Love*. New York: Ballantine Books, 1994.

Woititz, Janet. *Struggle for Intimacy.* Deerfield Beach, FL: Health Communications, 1988.

Wolf, Naomi. *The Beauty Myth.* New York: William Morrow & Co., 1991.

Woodman, Marion. *Addiction to Perfection.* Toronto: Inner City Books, 1982.

———. *The Pregnant Virgin: Psychological Transformation.* Toronto: Inner City Books, 1984.

———. *Conscious Femininity.* Toronto: Inner City Books, 1984.

Runes

The following short list is intended for those who wish to go more deeply into runic and related studies. Two books (Loyn and Elliott) contain more extensive and scholarly bibliographies.

Some authors (Bates, Branston, Crossley-Holland, Magnusson, Simpson and Wilson) are included for those who want to learn more about the Viking and Anglo-Saxon world.

Bates, Brian. *The Way of Wyrd.* London: Century Publishing, 1983.

Blum, Ralph H. *The Book of Runes: Tenth Anniversary Edition.* New York: St. Martin's Press, 1993.

———. *The Book of RuneCards.* New York: St. Martin's Press, 1989.

———. *Rune Play.* New York: St. Martin's Press, 1985.

Branston, Brian. *The Lost Gods of England.* London: Thames & Hudson, 1957.

Crossley-Holland, Kevin. *The Norse Myths.* New York: Pantheon Books, 1980.

Elliott, Ralph W. V. *Runes: An Introduction.* Manchester: Manchester University Press, 1959; New York: Philosophical Library, 1959; revised 1989.

Jansson, Sven B. F. *The Runes of Sweden,* trans. Peter Foote. London: Phoenix House, 1962.

Loyn, H. R. *The Vikings in Britain.* New York: St. Martin's Press, 1977.

Magnusson, Magnus. *Hammer of the North*. London: Orbis Publishing, 1979.

Marsden, John. *The Fury of the Northmen*. New York: St. Martin's Press, 1993.

Osborn, Marijane, and Stella Longland. *Rune Games*. London: Routledge & Kegan Paul, 1982.

Page, R. I. *An Introduction to English Runes*. London: Methuen, 1973.

Simpson, Jacqueline. *The Viking World*. New York: St. Martin's Press, 1980.

Wilson, David. *The Vikings and Their Origins*. London: Thames & Hudson, 1970.

The Oracular Tradition

Jung, Carl G. *Synchronicity: An Acausal Connecting Principle*. Princeton, NJ: Princeton University Press, 1973.

Koestler, Arthur. *The Roots of Coincidence*. London: Hutchinson & Co., 1972.

Sams, Jamie. *Sacred Path Cards*. San Francisco: HarperCollins, 1990.

———, and David Carson. *The Medicine Cards*. Santa Fe, NM: Bear & Co., 1988.

Yoshikawa, Takeshi. *The Ki: An Ancient Oracle for Modern Times*. New York: St. Martin's Press, 1986.

About the Authors

Ralph H. Blum was born in 1932. He is the author of *The Book of Runes* (St. Martin's Press, 1982). Blum received a degree in Russian Studies from Harvard University. Following two years in Italy as a Fulbright Scholar, he returned to Harvard where he did graduate work in anthropology with grants from the National Science and Ford Foundations.

He and his wife, Jeanne Elizabeth Blum, author of *Woman Heal Thyself: An Ancient Healing System for Contemporary Women,* live in Malibu, California, and Haiku, Maui.

Susan Loughan was first trained as an investigative journalist and later as an educator. She received her B.A. from Sonoma State University and did graduate work on a grant from the Far West Laboratory for Educational Research and Development. As a developmental specialist, she taught for fifteen years, nine of those years at Santa Rosa Junior College in the field of developmental disabilities.

For the past thirty years, Loughan has been a healer specializing in all forms of abuse recovery. A prescription drug addict and survivor of childhood sexual abuse, she has participated in Recovery programs for close to fifteen years. Her deep love of the American Indian people has led her to spend the past three decades as a Human Rights activist.

She lives with her daughter, Wende, in Santa Fe, New Mexico.

The RuneWorks

The RuneWorks was established in 1983 as a resource for people working with the Viking Runes. Now, we at the RuneWorks are especially interested in hearing from you as you become familiar with the Healing Runes.

Any Oracle is only validated through use and practice. And since this new oracular instrument has only just been put into circulation, just "commissioned," so to speak, we want to learn of your experiences with the Healing Runes: How has the Oracle served you? Is there something lacking that you would like to see included? Have you suggestions to strengthen the Oracle, or to widen its array and increase its usefulness? Have any ideas for different spreads occurred to you?

The midwifing of Oracles is a function that can only be completed through wide community participation. Susan and I, and all those who have supported us, have done our part for the moment. What we need now are the responses and comments of many people.

The Healing Runes partake of an ancient and sacred tradition with roots in Scripture itself. The Oracle will do no mischief to your beliefs nor will it intervene between you and God. On that account, I have one story to share with you.

Soon after it was published, I took *The Book of Runes* to India to show to the Benedictine monk Father Bede Griffiths, who was living in Tamil Nadu in Southern India at the time. He kept the book and the stones for three days, then asked if he might have them. I was very pleased. I told him that my prayer life had grown stronger since I added the Runes to my spiritual practice, but that I was still a bit nervous about how religious people would regard the Oracle. Father Bede smiled sweetly and giving the bag a shake, said: "Well, you might say the Runes are just another means of calling home."

The Sacred is indivisible, faction-free and quite accessible to all who desire to communicate with the Divine.

Write to us—to Bronwyn Jones or to Susan or me—and let us know if you want to be placed on our mailing list and receive our catalogue. Bronwyn has been my literary partner for almost fifteen years. It is she who publishes The Rune-Works Catalogue. She also edited *The Book of Runes, Rune Play* and *The RuneCards.* If you are interested in obtaining any of those works, and are having difficulty finding them, or if you prefer to purchase additional copies (with or without stones or cards) directly through us, we will be happy to assist you.

You will find us—Bronwyn, Susan and me—at the following address. Do let us hear from you:

The RuneWorks
P.O. Box 1320
Venice, CA 90294
(310) 399-3755